MINING NEW GOLD—
MANAGING YOUR BUSINESS DATA
DATA MANAGEMENT FOR BUSINESS OWNERS

PENNY,
JEFFREY AND
GILLIAN GARBUS

authorHOUSE®

AuthorHouse™
1663 Liberty Drive
Bloomington, IN 47403
www.authorhouse.com
Phone: 1 (800) 839-8640

Published by AuthorHouse 09/01/2017

ISBN: 978-1-5462-0586-9 (sc)
ISBN: 978-1-5462-0585-2 (hc)
ISBN: 978-1-5462-0587-6 (e)

Library of Congress Control Number: 2017913385

Print information available on the last page.

Any people depicted in stock imagery provided by Thinkstock are models, and such images are being used for illustrative purposes only. Certain stock imagery © Thinkstock.

This book is printed on acid-free paper.

Contents

Mining New Gold: Data Management

Data Management For Business Owners

Dear Reader,

I know you are overworked, stressing about your business not growing fast enough and worried it will grow so fast you can't keep up with the workload and system changes to keep clients happy. At different times, you need to make sure specific reports run accurately and quickly to meet deadlines from government agencies, and your CIO and CFO who need the numbers crunched. Meanwhile, you have bug fixes, maintenance on your systems and HIPAA and Sarbanes Oxley compliance. Let's not forget security issues as well. Every day there seems to be a new hack you must watch and defend against.

On top of all this, your budget has to be limited, and staff is overworked and stressed no matter how dedicated.

This book is intended to help you look at your environment in a new light and to look at data to guide you. You should review rules and regulations, the performance, and the reporting, now and as the data ages. Consider its values and business rules to help clean up the mess. Your data is a gold mine. Together, we can help change the perspective to help you come up with a plan to protect it.

Jeff and Penny Garbus have worked with companies across most verticals and most IT department sizes. However, there are issues they all share.

1. The data they are responsible for is often more precious than realized until they can't access it. They assume, just like the sun rises and moon sets every day, the data will always be there, accessible, accurate and performing efficiently.
2. They sometimes don't realize how much work is involved in maintaining the data environments and how important it is to develop proper maintenance plans
3. Maintenance is only the beginning. Following up with disaster recovery plans and ensuring those plans are validated is vital to success when something goes wrong.

We believe this would be the best way to help business leaders understand processes. Some of the highlights of our careers have been helping businesses save jobs, become more profitable and in mentoring IT teams. We enjoy sharing our knowledge and believe an educated client is a better one.

Chapter 1

New Gold/Data Management for Business

New Gold

Just as gold is a raw material for coins, jewelry, and watches, so too can data be viewed as the raw material from which money is obtained. In fact, a good definition of data is "facts or figures from which a conclusion can be made, giving the data perceived value by the author and the audience." Data information and statistics are often misunderstood, just like fool's gold. I found the basis for this definition from the Statistics Canada website and polished it. [#1F]

Armies and families have killed each other over gold. At time of the gold rush, during 1848 - 1855 people were desperate to hold it, honor its value, and create wondrous things with it. Originally, our dollar and entire economy were based on gold. The gold standard became a mantra that meant excellence. Gold was a commodity protected by the government, there was a time government determined how much each person could have. [#2F]

As you move along in this book, you will see other similarities, like government regulations of gold as a resource and control of data. The government is turning to data mining to circumvent need for warrants. It purchases data from private companies to have ready access. The US Supreme Court has tried these cases and determined an individual has no reasonable expectations of privacy to data that is held, managed, or maintained by a third party. Therefore, the Fourth Amendment does not protect an individual's data that reside in the public domain. Social media and other public venues are able to provide access to the government when asked, and no warrants or other legal procedures are necessary. Hackers (i.e., robbers) are stealing data, reselling it, releasing to the public, and holding it for ransom. If the dark net knows data has value, then we need to protect it.

In this new millennium, data is controlled, regulated, and hoarded; ownership is given to the individual so the entity cannot share it and must protect individual data through regulation reporting, security compliance, and suggested methodologies for proper management. The United States and governments throughout the world are dictating to companies how they must protect data.

For example, in 1998, the United Kingdom enacted the Data Protection Act, which states sensitive personal data cannot be transferred into a non-European Union country unless that country has the means to protect the sensitive data. Although we have our own HIPAA laws to protect individual's health data, we do not have legislation to protect the data as tightly as the European Union. [#3F]

Since many companies are global and in the United States laws control healthcare-related information, companies that are not generally regulated must jump through regulatory hoops to continue doing business in the United Kingdom.

Case Summary

Take a company that runs software for schools worldwide. This company might run applications and store the production data inside the United Kingdom, but its backups might go to a colocation site outside the United Kingdom. Secondly, every vendor who could touch any of the related environments had to be audited by the United Kingdom, even if the people, database, and environment they worked on was in the

United States because the individuals who own the end data lived in the United Kingdom.

The ownership and protection of each individual's data "nugget" supersedes the right and privileges of the company that houses, stores, administers, and maintains the data. That makes it an interesting statement about this economy. A business owns the data as a whole with all integral parts of the sale or service, but in the end, the business must protect the nuggets to protect the rights of the individual and incur costs for all aspects of that protection.

The cost of protecting personal information is high for companies today. They have to provide security in the form of software, firewalls, processes, and audit controls to make sure no one accessed the personal information data. The personal information data is what in many circumstances inherently adds value to the data.

Providing access but limiting details to each user is another process that causes pain points and cost overruns in projects and data management. We haven't even talked about performance and direct user access costs. How you need to deliver the data—through fax, e-mails, web portals, mobile devices, videos, images, or telephonic or voice devices—should be considered.

As access to data grows and personal information becomes more detailed, government agencies will become more critical of how data is protected. The data stream causes corporations to follow protocols to protect their data and to protect rights and privileges of the data owner. The government will manipulate the way businesses grow, spend money, and hire professionals.

This has created a time when data might be as important as any other commodity but will need to be protected as your company's success depends on keeping it in the vault.

Summary

Data is becoming more relevant in the world around us. Protecting someone's data and ensuring it will be accessible are causing more regulations throughout the world.

Data is becoming so valuable that in the next chapters you will be able to create entire markets around preparing, massaging, and analyzing data that could be stored in your systems.

Chapter 2

Why Do I Protect It?

Got Data? Protect It

If you have data, then your business data management problems are directly correlated to the type of and amount you are managing. If you own a restaurant, you have to protect the credit card transactions that are handled through your point-of-sale, or POS, software. The POS is responsible for security, maintenance, and management of that data. After you set up the POS, check the background of anyone who handles transactions and set up guidelines for properly handling the credit card and entering the transaction in the POS. If you do this, you are probably safe from the rest of the security requirements for credit card transactions.

The rest of your data consists of inventory and sales analysis of beverages and food, including to whom and when it was served. With this data, you can capture what customers like and don't like. Seasonal specialties or just preferences and how you might use that data analysis can increase sales or improve quality of your product. It also can improve ordering, inventory, and delivery schedule.

If you own one restaurant, you might be able to handle this data in spreadsheets or a small database/application system. If you own thousands of restaurants across continents, then you have a different problem. You have inventory control per thousands, timeline issues, customs, and possibly different offerings, depending on the restaurant location. Your data analysis must be tighter and better thought out. Applications and real-time data strategies need to be met as opposed to the data warehousing process where you can analyze data over dozens of seasons and years. Your data issues just became geometrically magnified. Your data access needs are no longer met with a simple solution. Now you have database performance problems as well as server and database relationship issues.

Now change the restaurant to an insurance company. Take away inventory and add HIPAA, SOC, and SarBox (Sarbanes-Oxley Act) compliance, users such as doctors, labs, patients, nurses, and drugstores, as well as state and federal compliance, and you kind of own the data. But patients are the legal owners. If you don't protect that data, you are potentially out of business. You not only need to secure it against the hacker but you must back it up and maintain and protect it from corruption. If you lose or share it, someone can stake a claim to that data and force you to defend the claim.[3]

Ownership is key. It no longer can be determined by the finders-keepers rule or the last one to touch data owns it. Data is not exclusively yours, but it is yours to protect and value.

Data can be used to enhance the value of your companies and can be used to market importance in your industry. It can be manipulated to provide information that will help grow your companies and find ways to improve service or products to entice customers.

The historical data, in terms of pattern recognition and usage, can sometimes be as important as today's data when trying to find a path forward. After a while, it can age and the validity can be compromised, maybe because in the past reports weren't as detailed as they are now or products have changed so much the target audience also has changed.

Historical data for a restaurant could track favorites by season. It seems to reason that in winter months, folks crave richer, warmer foods. However, with New Year's resolutions, salads and vegetables might have a high selling season in January. The data can help provide information as to what foods to stock up on, saving spoilage fees. Also, you might want to create coupons that match the tastes of customers during different seasons to lure them from competitors.

Creating social media campaigns that match these trends is another way to create a closer relationship with clients by sharing with them your understanding of their dietary wants for good health.

I believe we often look into the data with rose-colored glasses instead of taking a critical view. When reviewing data, if we allow the data to create new paths, we might gain better insight as to our own paths forward. These paths might help us design better products and services that push us past competitors.

Case Summary

In an article in *Small Business Chron*, the authors discuss thoughts I would like to share.[#4b] Managers spend about two hours researching data per day. Often that data can be erroneous, incomplete, or invalid because it is disconnected. Or it does not have history or details for full query or business analysis or is disjointed because of missing facts. Also, data can be disparate, saved in different systems, databases, and environments, making it hard to get the data reestablished usefully.

In our case, we create client reports that track work efforts so we can prove we have completed activities, have approval for those activities, and document time and effort spent to complete the work. Here are issues we deal with to make sure data is processed to provide honest, factual report for clients:

1. Ensure processes and procedures are easy for users to follow.
2. Create an interface with guidelines but allows the user to easily do the data entry freeform so the order of entry does not matter. Therefore, we cannot create rules that require data to be entered in any order nor can we create a status that limits actions.
3. Once the data is entered we need to be able to create reports that provide accurate data and add accurate hours so that time

cannot be added twice should the work cross weeks or months, affecting billing.

This seems to be so easy you will say: "What's the problem?" However, how do you make sure a task that stays open across billing statements and hours is added as you go? How do you make sure hours are not billed twice? Then how do you make sure you are able to bill at the end? When hours are limited by a statement of work you can't add up all hours at the end because you need to track as you bill to make sure you don't go over.

Every time we add more details to our activities logs we need to review the reports to make sure rules haven't been broken that would cause billing issues. Also, if reports are run asking different questions you want to be sure data maps accordingly. Sometimes the query itself and how you ask it, what date types and ranges are chosen and other conditions can skew the data. Until both queries are analyzed, you may not understand why data doesn't map.

If you can, hire a Business Intelligence expert or purchase a BI tool. If first you get the data collection right, the data restructured through a business intelligence tool can improve the bottom line. Your bottom line can be impacted through small changes that improve usability, quality, intelligence, easy remote access and sales mobility. Accurate data is an important customer service strategy.

For example, the only thing that bugs me about Amazon is I might pay extra expecting to get two-day shipping. However, their application usually fails to note the processing of my purchase can take 5-10 days, negating my extra costs in paying for the upgraded delivery charge. To me, Amazon's application should note when my product won't come within two days because it does not accurately inform the customer.

In a study from the University of Texas in 2010, researchers found the average company could increase annual sales per employee by 14.4 percent if it increased stability of its data by 10 percent. For the average Fortune 1000 company in the study, this amounted to a potential increase in productivity of $55,900 per employee. Investment in effective and efficient methods of transforming data into usable business intelligence will pay dividends. [#2F]

Imagine the increase in customer satisfaction that would result should the data be so accurate the client could know the time a package would land on the doorstep.

Summary

Basically, you protect data for the company's best interest. That means meeting regulation standards and protecting against lawsuits from individuals who are related to the data.

Also the data itself has historical and possible cash value if you can provide the data in a manner that interests prospects. Protecting the data can mean protection not only for the bottom line but could affect your future as well.

Chapter 3

How Important is Your Data?

Your data is as important as you believe so. But consider this: Statistically, 65 percent of companies that suffer catastrophic data loss close their doors. You must not only consider how precious the regulatory agencies believe your data is to the individual, but you have to consider how precious the data is for your company.

Data is important depending on how you use it and how much time and money is spent to protect it. If you spend little protecting data, you have given data little value. This value had better reflect the real value of the data, however. You don't want to find out one day you have been disconnected from the data running your business.

Ask yourself this: "What happens if I lose all my data tomorrow?" If you reply, "I move on, nothing much will happen to my job, my company or my clients," you could be in denial. If this question panics you, then do something about it. If your answer is "I have backups, redundant systems, proper restore procedures and my team has a full disaster recovery process in place, and has practiced and evaluated these procedures on a timely basis" then you not only have recognized value of your data, you understand the role of data in today's marketplace.

We worked with a medical insurance provider company, which found it had a corrupted database, and no restorable backups newer than six months old. The backups had been corrupted before anyone noticed the issues. If we had not managed to pull data from the corrupted database, 4,000 workers would have been looking for employment elsewhere that week.

This company spent two weeks, praying the data could be recovered. Patient data that was saved may have saved thousands of lives as well. Today, no one can afford to be cavalier about data. The truth is, if it doesn't mean much to you, check regulations because you will find those who believes data matters. The tragedy of data loss may not end when you close your doors. Lawsuits and regulatory agencies can make your life a nightmare if you fail to understand, develop and follow processes that protect regulated data.

Sometimes being out of compliance means you are not following industry-standard best-business practices to manage data. It may be as simple as making sure the environment is being watched for breaches, capacity issues and being held with software and hardware in compliance with vendors. We had a new medical provider who didn't realize by not having proper monitoring and maintenance jobs set up they could be fined for not following Healthcare Privacy and Portability Act procedures. Those procedures regulate requirements to ensure data is protected through professional and proper data management. The jobs they needed to have set up were successful backup processes, database integrity and capacity checks, and server availability, or heartbeat checks. Once these jobs were set up they were in line with regulations. Processes required by HIPAA guidelines were immediately set up and within 24 hours the environment was compliant.

Case Summary

There is a small startup. The startup knew HIPAA compliance meant having proper security protocols, including logins, passwords, roles, hiding private data when not needed by the user, backing up databases and providing proper reporting to regulators. What they did not know; they were out of compliance because they did not have a maintenance plan designed and put in place. The startup also did not have the recommended operating system and database version patches for security put in place by specific software vendors needed for their environment. They simply didn't have time nor experience to do all this work.

If you can't afford to buy experience, lease it.

Summary

In the end your data is as important as you decide it should be. You should evaluate data, consider what a loss of the data would mean to your company and from there start building a plan to protect it.

Remember, 65 percent of companies that suffer catastrophic data loss will close their doors. What would happen if you lost your data? How long would it take to recover this information? Is it even possible to rebuild it? Think of what it would take to rebuild your Outlook contacts? What if tomorrow your Outlook file was corrupted and you had to rebuild data from scratch? Now multiply those concerns into millions of rows of data sitting in your databases today.

How much data can I afford to lose?

Let's answer this by asking you to think about this question: How much data can you afford to lose?

Is the answer one year's worth? Or is it one month, a week, a day or an hour, minutes or seconds?

If the answer is an entire year, or greater, then stop reading. You have more important things to do than read this book. If you don't know, then let's think about a few things.

If you lost all of your data for the last hour, day or week, can you reconstruct it and get back to business? If the answer is yes, then skip to the next paragraph. Would reconstructing that data mean new sales goals are not met or you just walked into compliance issues? As soon as you say reconstructing the data hits your company's bottom line or could send you on a legal journey, then you need to make sure the data is protected. If you have not thought of data in relation to your financial well-being don't feel bad; you are not alone. This also doesn't mean it's because you are a small business or not intelligent. It just means you have not had a moment to contemplate this issue. Sometimes you are so busy with your business you don't have time to worry about small stuff, the bits and bytes of your data and how relevant it is to longevity of your business.

So you have decided you need to make sure you do not lose more data than you can afford.

How much of the data is important? How much has value to the company? How long do you have to keep data?

Which would be worse: losing all your data or losing all the money in the payroll account?

Which is easier to get back if stolen? Does stolen mean you are not only out of business, but you lose your licensing and find yourself being investigated by agencies for negligence?

Which will cause a class action? If you have been hacked because of improper security protocols or if you failed to have professional standard security processes?

Data is like gold; it can be traded, it is the base for creation of many products, and if you lose it you lose money. How much control do you want to have of your data? There are predators after your data and they prey on your willingness to get it back. Some of these questions will be answered by ever-changing government regulations. In one industry we worked in, the government was famous for creating new regulations and backdating them by 18 months.

However, it is good to review these questions every year. Keeping this data is expensive. Some companies keep so much data for such a long time they forget what and where it was stored, and whether it is relevant. They continue to pay for storage of the old data and buy more storage without doing a spring time cleanout. So as you are analyzing, don't assume everything is important. Cleaning out old data could save you money.

Make sure you keep old backups. If you back up every hour, make sure you keep staged backups. If you are not certain how many to keep, check with regulatory guidelines in your industry or service level agreement that was promised customers as to how long you need to keep backups. In the end make sure you have them staged so you can get back to a point in time if the backup is corrupted. One backup is not enough. You need to stage them, get them offsite, preferably out of region, and test them periodically to make sure backups are restorable. One of the worst false promises you can make is to believe you are safe because of backups.

Case Summary

A mid-level company believed they had everything in place to ensure data was safe. Then one day the data was corrupted. They had not noticed until the data was unusable, so the corruption had existed for a while. They believed they were protected because they backed up the database daily. What happened was the data had been corrupted for a long time and the backups were corrupted as well. They never tested their restore process. Because the restore process was never tested, they had not realized there were steps and procedures missing and the backups were useless. Thousands of jobs were at stake.

Summary

Can you really afford to lose even a small amount of data? If you lost all transactions in the past 15 minutes would you be able to recover the data in less than a day? If it was lost what would that cost in revenue, lawsuits or fines? You should begin self-analysis to design data protection processes and procedures. From here define your needs and then talk with IT staff to ensure all agree business data protection needs match data recovery and protection strategies.

Chapter 4

What Goes in the Vault?

What data do you archive? Or what data do you keep in your vault for long-term storage?

Regulations and service level agreements could determine some of the decisions as to what data you should keep in long-term storage. After that has been determined, you might want to look at your own company's users for answers. I will bet your sales and marketing team or researchers are going to want to hoard more data than your accountants or inventory control managers. This is where you have to look through the weeds. How much of the data is valuable as time passes? For example, will real-time aspects of who recorded the purchase of 20 widgets and how the sales were processed be useful later? Or is just the type, color, version of the widget, who sold and purchased it and when the transactions took place the most important aspects? If so then you can strip out the unnecessary data and only keep the data vital to statistical research you may need for insight into your market.

It is not always necessary to put all data and databases into a vault. Analyzing what should go into the vault can save you in hardware and maintenance costs. For example, there is a lot of metadata (data about the data) shared and stored about the hard data you will want to store. You may want to review that metadata to see if it is necessary to keep in your data warehouse or long-term vault. For example, if you have data about who bought what product from you on a certain date that all seems to be good data to store. But do you need to know who keyed in the data, what IP address they used and other user-related code. This may be something you want to investigate and search later but it also could be basically garbage data that can be kept from the warehouse.

How long do you need to keep old data?

In addition to the regulations you must adhere to, you should take a few moments to discuss with your team what data you need to keep and what data (even metadata) you can get rid of after a period of time. Some data is necessary to keep in order to collect historical points if only to compare your business' performance decade over decade. Other data, like who entered an order for 4,000 widgets and when, may not be important so you may be able to cleanse some of the related metadata but keep specific data to run reports year over year, saving time and space.

Sit down with users and your CFO, CIO and compliance officer to discuss what data you need to save and create a strategy to purge old unused data. Create and carry out a strategy with these team members, with rules. If you are not sure, back up or archive some of the data in a way it can be brought back into the database.

Case Study

Often we have clients who hire us because they just don't have time for all the grunt work. Sometimes the database and applications have been stored so long no one is sure what is valuable and what is not. After hiring us, we have been able to come through with monitoring and monthly analysis that helps determine living active data from old inactive data. Then we worked with the client to map unusable to usable data. And we could remove or archive old inactive environments off production environments, saving them millions in maintenance and storage costs. The work was tedious and took team effort but in the end it was a profitable process for our client.

Summary

Basically, reviewing what you want to keep for long-term storage is important. You don't want to spend time and resources managing this data for decades.

On the other hand, you don't want to throw away anything that could be of value later. You may want to ask impossible questions to see what you get from your data. There may be surprising results as to how you can re-align the information and find a market for it or to create algorithms for insights about clients, products and markets you never imagined you could get from data. We suggest once a year you should review the database and entire data environment schema and create a wish list to see what you might like to ask your systems. The answers may surprise you. Also, there are tools that can be bought to up to speed with the investigation phase of this exercise.

Spring clean your data

Regularly cleanse your data as you would do spring cleaning at home or your closet after you lose weight.

After talking with users, the CIO, CFO and regulatory members, business directors then present your project with rules and suggestions to your IT staff for a plan to start cleaning out data. At this time, you may want to ask the IT staff to create a schema for each physical server on what databases, applications and software is housed there.

There may be old third-party software on servers you have never used, or no longer use, stored on your devices. This may be a good time to weed out these items and gain needed space. Also you may have some in-house applications you built a decade or more ago that have been replaced with new systems you can identify and either remove from production environments and store in cheaper devices or delete altogether.

The reason I bring all this up is to help you consider approaching data from this perspective. How much of the data is your company emotionally tied too? What data can you live without? We have a couple of large retail clients. They have old databases and data they are not sure which, if any, applications touch them. They are not sure if the data is used. But they hold onto these databases like each one has value. (Tip: If you are unsure whether people are accessing a database, try cautiously disconnecting it for a while.)

Part of the spring cleaning plan should be to review a couple of these databases for a year or a quarter. Look to see if there are new rows of data; look at the database metadata to see when was the last time a user accessed the data, then determine if the database should be kept or if you can at least archive the databases onto lower cost storage instead of keeping them on active devices. From this point look at the used applications, databases and software to make sure all are pointing to correct devices, databases and software versions. You may discover unused databases at this point and then decide whether to archive those databases, delete or keep them on your production servers.

If your company is a legacy company or if you have bought and sold parts of your business, this may be a challenge. So, scheduling a regular cleanout session quarterly or twice a year may help manage the workload without interfering with your day-to-day business development needs. There are organizations with software that can help you map out what is being stored on your hardware and provide you with reports.

Cost savings

When we have reviewed environments after being brought on to design and develop maintenance strategies, we have found some of the databases empty and never used. This also can help cut down on software licensing costs from database server licenses to all types of management and security licensing used to manage old or empty databases.

Once you map databases, data and applications, and you know those in use and those not, you can decide which are needed to keep in production environments, choosing the ones you want to archive and possibly remove others.

You not only will have more space on your servers and storage devices but be able to remove these databases from your backups, and from maintenance and audit processes. This will save money on monitoring software for your backups. Remember backups can be staged so you may get a lot of space, software and personnel time freed up by just not having to manage the backups.

If you have auditing requirements, you will save on possible software, personnel hours and reporting time for auditing management of unused data. Add maintenance management, such as integrity and job failure checks, space and performance analysis, and you saved personnel time. Of course, each time you clean up your environment then your savings continue to grow and the cleanup and discovery processes become a lighter load. The trick is to plan and begin this process. Just like spring cleaning at home, you eventually get through it and life is more organized.

By looking at your IT budget you can do the math to determine whether you should start this process. If your hardware costs are $2 million, and, let's say, technical personnel costs are $500,000, software is $1 million and once you clean up environments you release 10 percent of the workload, then your savings could be 10 percent of each cost structure (between hardware, software and personnel time costs) saving $200,000-$300,000 for your overall budget. This can affect your hiring and growth of your business.

If you are unsure whether this is worth the effort, try reviewing one physical server. Don't do the work, just do the analysis and review what data, applications and software is being stored and what you presume is unused. If you see value to the review exercise, start planning to do the cleanup. If possible, schedule it during a slow business season.

There are software and service providers who will do this investigation if you don't have staff to manage it. Therefore, you may want to contract out the service.

Case Summaries

A financial organization that had purchased a company with legacy applications, software and data, had held, migrated and was maintaining dozens of environments with more than 5 percent unusable items on servers. They were able to clean up the environments and save enough space to put off purchasing more hardware and saved on software licenses for the next two years. A consulting company was hired to clean up the environment. They were able to recoup enough from the expense of hiring a consulting company for this project to pay for consulting fees, and saved an additional 25 percent in hardware maintenance costs and upgrades the first year.

A manufacturing client was brought on board last year. The client had more than 50 servers and each server had hundreds of databases. Many of the databases were not in use. They were used with applications that had been turned off in some cases five or more years ago. The client was backing up, and paying for software and hardware maintenance for these databases. They were paying for normal maintenance and capacity checks by staff. They were storing data and paying for that storage year over year. Then, they added in costs of the backups for that data. Since they properly staged their backups, they had 4–5 stored backups per database they were not only storing but paying folks to maintain them.

The costs of taking care of these old databases ran into the millions. Once we started to clean house we were able to archive data on other devices. We could open up space on their production servers. Plus, we reduced staff time which freed them up and our team, allowing all to concentrate on processes and data that would help them grow their business. The effort to get this done was time consuming and frustrating, but rewards would be continual in cost savings in years to come.

Summary

Creating a clean house regimen for your environment may be daunting, especially if you have dozens or hundreds of servers with hundreds of databases on each server. However, if you create a project plan and work on this in segments, you will probably find patterns that will help you get the cleanup done faster than you anticipated as you work through the process.

For example, you may have redundant stored databases. Let's say a decade ago you had an old database used for accounting, then you purchased a tool and imported all the data into the tools database. All this time you have been keeping not only the original accounting database but backups as well.

Or what if there was an old application that touched different databases and entire systems were replaced? Well, map out the application, check age of the data and you can at least clear this data from your production environments, storing the data in your data warehouse if you want it long term. Now you no longer need to maintain, manage and store all of it on a month-to-month or week-to-week process.

We hope you see value in doing this while reading this chapter or you are able to say: "Been there, done that. Now send me a free t-shirt."

Chapter 5

How Data is Driving Technology Today

Is data driving technology or is technology creating a higher value for data?

Access to data is from anywhere. Society is addicted to data. We expect information fast, 24 hours, from any device and at voice request. The more we get, the more we want.

We are a society addicted to knowing what is going on in the world and devices can wake us up if we have alerts.

Did technology make us addicts or did our need for data cause technology to advance? It appears this addiction has been fed to us through the marketplace and our desire for immediate stimulus brought on by emotional push and pull from the data.

The immediacy of data-driven satisfaction may have started with Federal Express and fax machines. For the first time, we were able to get documents signed and delivered in lightning speed without having to send a courier by plane, train or automobile.

Then Internet showed up. We had Comcast Messenger, we had RAZ server messages that were not-so-instant messaging that gave birth to our new world of instant creative thoughtful data exchanges.

It is hard to remember everyone sitting around after dinner at night, watching Walter Cronkite tell us who won the election, who landed on the moon or offering news of the war.

Humans hunger for information and technology feeds our curiosity.

But technology also is an enabler feeding our addiction for information.

Data is driving our world in many ways, from mobile advances to expectations of being able to use those devices anytime and anywhere. We are no longer tied to phones. We can pocket phones and weed through messages and calls that show on our wrists. While sitting at a meeting, we can read the text and voice mail, and with little interruption in our conversations, we can decide whether the meeting is more important than the disrupting call.

The more precious the data, the more precious our time. We are connected to each other all the time.

Technology and Data: Who drives who?

Does our craving cause changes in technology or does the technology create the desire and need for data?

In our society, we can imagine the most remarkable things. Do you remember riding in The Walt Disney Future World ride as a child and imagining being able to see your dad or grandma's face to show them your report card? Now you can talk to anyone whether you know them or not in many ways over the internet. This just adds sugar to our cake and we want more. We demand to have 4G access with our data plans. We want unlimited data all the time from anywhere. Gone are the days when we used to pay roaming charges because we left our neighborhoods to speak with someone over the phone. We are demanding more and we want it all cheaper.

I Tunes and now Alexa allows us to listen to music by just clearly speaking and requesting our favorite songs from our favorite artists. Now Google will allow us to take a picture, through imaging recognition and GPS information. Google will tell us details about buildings, places in the building, history of the building and the community. Google will also tell us about pictures of flora and fauna. We will know the name of a bird are flower as we take our mental meditative walks through the forest. The data we will have at our fingertips will be astounding. We may never be truly alone again, unless we unplug.

In business, we want data and we want it now. We need it to be accurate and we need it consistently faster. If we don't demand this of ourselves our clients will go elsewhere and the bottom line will feel the pain. People will expect the information and they won't want to wait even seconds for it. Instant knowledge transfer is the expectation. Time wasting is no longer allowed if we want to keep our customers.

How big data is changing healthcare

Imagine a health care plan created just for you. Imagine if a doctor could see your medical history, plus plotting your blood type, weight, ethnicity, lifestyle and gender and then match up your disease or condition into a data construct that will provide the most effective healthcare strategy for you. Which drugs should work the best for you; which should you shy away from? We are close to being able to have this data at medical providers' fingertips to help map out a healthcare plan specific for you, taking out guesswork and providing effective and efficient care.

Mapping a health matrix supports individual needs. We can track our personal health goals. We can track what we eat, how much we drink and our social happiness. Eventually we could monitor our moods, and track insulin, cholesterol and blood pressure. Imagine if all this data could be ported (in highly secure transactions) to our doctors who not only treat us when we are ill but use this data to keep us well. Imagine savings in emergency room care and pharmaceutical costs. Prescriptions don't go unused or they don't get abused. We could manage the amount of opioids we can use to become not addicted. We don't rush to the emergency room for indigestion but head over when it could be angina or a stroke.

The mobility of personal data could be the answer to health care savings should the medical community prepare for its onslaught, and administration and analysis of that data through smart algorithms and medical knowledge for personal medical tracking teams. Doctors can cross-share the information to prevent over-medication and they can, as a team, prevent emergency care responses by just keeping their patients on track. If the patient chooses not to stay on track, there could be other medical teams such as therapists and home health trainers who could be solicited to discern why. New mobile data devices can bring about a revolution in health care and also prevent doctor-free zones. Areas where there are medical shortages could provide secondary community coverage from a medical team anywhere in the world. [#5F]

How big data is changing the world

A Wall Street Journal article in 2013 discusses applications for Big Data that changed the value of multiple businesses. One such business it cited was Zynga, best known for Farmville, which collects over 25 terabytes a day from its games. This is enough data to fill 1,000 blue ray discs. Zynga uses this data for quality assurance and helps it devise features and strategies for their next generation of games [#6F]

The more data you can collect from your clients the better you will be able to build your products and services to meet their needs. This will affect your market share, growth trajectory and bottom line.

Case Summary

The same Wall Street article presents a case where a hotel chain was able to glean so much information about their client's stays and habits, the company used social media to come up with campaigns that were focused on individuals, raising conversion rates of the marketing campaigns 35 percent higher than previous ones.

Marketing and sales tools are an example. We have used marketing tools to reach target markets. Some had a lot of missing data, or old data, both of which were useless. Our tool provides not only nearly 90 percent or better data accuracy but if we get a mailed item returned for insufficient or incomplete address, we can request a data update. Within 48 hours the data will be corrected.

If we pay for ability to connect with our target then the data needs to be accurate. We don't even have to mention this when it comes to personal, financial or medical data stored in hospitals and doctor offices. What if you went to the hospital and were billed for treatments or tests you never received? First, when this happens it is almost impossible to get the billing cleaned up; secondly, you get dunning calls until it can. While you are dealing with an illness you can be dealing with a medical bill with correct and incorrect charges.

The need for service providers to have processes that verify data, and to prove and correct errant data, is needed not only for customer satisfaction but to follow regulatory and in-house compliance to ensure proper delivery of services, record-keeping and business practices. There is a game in the malls. It allows players, at intervals, to ask a question that vendors in the mall would like to ask but wanting people to fill out surveys is not effective. Instead, the player is enticed to answer questions. Since they are being rewarded, I wonder if answers are more honest plus there is no person to judge answers so you may be able to collect more reliable information in this manner.

Yes, both scenarios are invasive but the data about us is out there being used by promoters and research analysts. It is time for that data to work for us.

The more data is available and more we have access, the more technology will change and grow to make use of the data. We will find new methods of access. We can see more data processing power, not to mention streaming data, on a watch today than in the first Apollo spacecraft in 1965. Maybe the need for data is driven by curiosity, and we are using technology to feed the curiosity. Or maybe technology is getting us addicted to data. Either way, we are a data-driven world.

Consider this fact: In 2002 one in 10 people owned a cell phone in sub-Saharan Africa. In 2016, 83 percent of the people own a cell phone. Smart phones are widely in use. This region went to cell phones and skipped landline phone usage; it went straight to the digital age. They use the phones just as we do, for news, banking, and social media access, bringing us closer to each other. The more we get to know each other, the more we find we are alike. [#7F]

About 2.5 million cell phones have been smuggled into North Korea. Drones have been dropping SD (secure Digital) cards and flash drives to North Koreans because people are hungry for information from the outside. The sponsor of the drops hopes the information will one day help free this country.

Summary

Society is addicted to data. Data, access and having faster and typing-free access like SIRI and Alexa is bringing the world closer every day. One day Alexa may be able to determine our needs and provide data or services automatically. She could sense the kitchen light and coffee pot go on in the morning and know I would like to hear a weather, traffic and local news report to determine how to start my day. In the future, data will only get more personalized and accessible. That accessibility, however, is a double-edged sword. Although the efficiency allows people to get work finished faster, it also makes employees more accessible to employers, so the work never really ends.

Chapter 6

Security, Hiring Protection?

The U.S government said in "Protecting Your Networks from Ransomware" more than 4,000 ransomware attacks have occurred daily since the start of 2016. The attacks in 2016 were four times higher than in 2015. [#8F]

Most attacks are against financial, medical and retail business sectors. The ransoms are usually under $1,000 and most companies pay it. Attackers prefer payment through bitcoin which cannot be traced. However, in some cases the data and files are not completely freed up and some attackers will hold out until more money is paid. The worst scenario occurs when the attacker has so completely destroyed data files and infected hard drives they are unable to get back your data. The costs can run into thousands or millions to get a company up and running again.

The best way to protect yourself is to set up the proper security and off-site backups.

There are two basic types of ransomware. The first is locker room ransomware which basically locks you out of applications and processes on your computer. Locker room access is not necessarily an encryption virus. It may just create a barrier between you and the computer's interface so the only thing you can do is see the ransomware attack screen which requests payment to release your computer. This type of ransomware uses threatening fake messages and tries to look like you have done something wrong. That's why law enforcement is knocking on your door.

It uses threatening images and is more of a psychological scare tactic; this ransomware can be cleansed from your computer and personal files restored. Also, virus protection services will be able to detect it and you can work with a provider to get rid of the ransomware should it attack undetected by the virus protection or firewall software.

It is best to consider paying for virus protection. Do research and make sure you are purchasing from a known brand. Be careful of virus protection software that appears magically through an email and declares it has found a virus. If you don't recognize the brand, ignore the findings. Run your trusted provider's processes. Sometimes viruses come in looking like they are doing you a favor finding viruses on your computer but they are the virus. I had virus protection software that would interrupt me every few seconds while I was working on my computer, telling me I had a virus. I had to run my actual purchased virus protection software, telling it to get rid of these files and email.

The second type of ransomware is a data lock or file encryption ransomware. This virus enters, encrypts and renames your files so you have no access and you can't recognize the files. Renaming takes away their file extension as well as the name you created them with. This type of ransomware works more stealth-like than the others. It creeps quietly until all files are encrypted, then it allows itself to be known. The author demands payment to release your computer from control. They typically ask for payment by bitcoin. The computer will continue to work but files that are locked down will not be accessible. However, they use threatening messaging to encourage prompt ransom payment by saying the key for de-encryption will be deleted and lost forever if payment is not received within a specific time period.

The first thing to consider is to make sure hardware and software are protected with firewalls and software that scans the environment for worms, harmful attachments and attacks.

The second tier will be to set up procedures and protocols for data access. It is important to make sure access to data is limited by setting up rules and roles in the database. For example, the system administrator role should be handed out to a limited number of people, who should not be sharing login information with each other.

Many environments are too lax with limiting access and controlling database environment. If you are not sure of your environment rules, review them. Then consider what processes you need to complete when employees leave. You need to make sure access is taken away and passwords are changed. Also you should consider encrypting data as it comes in and out of your environment.

Data encryption

Data is encrypted to keep its contents protected from prying eyes.

First, let's make sure we're on the same page from a terminology and process standpoint.

There are two basic components to data encryption: Encryption, where we store and protect data, and decryption, with which we retrieve and unscramble data.

On the encryption side, you need to be able to create and manage an encryption key, as well as to set permissions for logins who should have access. On the decryption side, you need to be able to transparently select from appropriate columns.

Data encryption meets both needs in data security: It protects data from friendly eyes, as well as unfriendly eyes, who have perhaps stolen a backup tape.

Encryption products have ability to create encryption keys and encrypt any other data in databases. This met a market need because there had been high-profile cases with stolen databases, leading to identity theft. Encryption has gotten better and easier, with ability to recover lost encryption keys, specify default values for data a user has no permission for, and additional datatypes that may be encrypted.

There are third-party products to perform the encryption, but performing the encryption at the database level is an improvement in performance and reduces need for a security tier. Don't we have enough tiers in our environments?

Many DBMS (Database Management Systems) manage security of keys by keeping them encrypted. There are two keys between user and the data: the column encryption key (CEK) and the key encryption key (KEK). The CEK encrypts data and users must have access before they can get to encrypted data. For security, it is stored in encrypted form. ASE (ASE SAP formerly known as Sybase Adaptive Server) encrypts the CEK with a KEK when you create or alter an encryption key. The KEK also is used to decrypt the CEK before you can access decrypted data. The KEK is derived internally from system encryption password, a user-specified password, or a login password, depending on how you specify the key's encryption.

Decrypting (querying) the data

Once the data has been encrypted using keys with user-defined passwords, things have to happen for a user to see data in the clear:

- You need select permission on the column to read the information, insert/update/delete permission (as appropriate) to modify the information.
- You need decrypt permission on the column to read (or if you're going to use it for comparison purposes in a query predicate). If you have select permission, and do not have decrypt permission, you're going to get either the default (if it has been applied) or a permissions error (if no default has been applied)[#1F]

Key copies enable users to access encrypted columns using their own copy of a single key. This provides accountability for data because a key copy is designated for an individual user with a private password known only to the user. Without knowledge of the passwords protecting the key and its copies, not even SA (systems administrator) can access the data.

Column encryption generally uses Advanced Encryption Standard (AES), with 128, 192, or 256-bit encryption key sizes. The longer the bit string, the more difficult it is for a hacker to decrypt. On the other hand, the more complicated the encryption, the more CPU resources will be taken up by the encryption/decryption algorithm.

Which level is right for you? That's a question for the site security officer. You should be aware most public, commercial products and projects are using 128-bit encryption, and the government uses that up to the SECRET level; Top Secret requires 192 or 256-bit encryption. How difficult is this to crack? It's been calculated cracking a 128-bit algorithm requires 2^{120} operations, which is not considered feasible [#9F]

That said, 128-bit encryption seems secure enough for most applications. But check with the security officer about your shop standard. If you go with a higher level, be sure to benchmark the effect of the higher level of encryption against CPU utilization.

If your application is hosted on the web, make sure you purchase an SSL certificate and an https URL rather than an http URL. This will add an extra layer of protection to your data and application to keep out unwanted access. The rule should be if you want to limit access to your application and have a login page, then your application should be using secure socket layer certificates and an https URL. The data then will be encrypted upon entering and sending the data. Not only will this keep folks from retrieving the data but from following holes into your systems.

Port Security

In the majority of systems, access requires authentication and authorization. Authentication asks, and answers, the question, "Are you who you say you are?" Authorization asks, and answers, the question, "Are you permitted to take the action you are trying for?"

Authentication is managed with a login and a password. The login gives the security system something to use as basis for lookup, and the password is used to verify the person logging in is supposed to. You'll find most systems have rules about mandatory password complexity. Without that, passwords are easy to guess or hack. Note if your password is less than 12 characters, it's likely not as secure as you believe it is. Brute force hacking tools, that are shareware/downloadable, will often figure out those passwords in seconds or minutes.

Authorization is generally managed with permissions inside the application. So, once you have logged in, the application permissions control what you can read or change.

Software bug fixes and updates.

As the system ages, you will find you will be provided bug fixes and sometimes upgrades for the software. Always review the bug fix, and install it in a development server first. Then test for everything from data integrity to performance before rolling up the bug fix. Keeping the software up to date is one key in protecting data. Try to keep your full environment in compliance. Software is aged out by vendors and if you have a corruption in an old database caused by a vendor software issue they will not help you once they have determined they are ending support for a particular version of the software.

The best way to keep data protected is to make sure the environment is kept healthy, so maintaining the software and hardware supported by the vendor adds a team that can help you when something bad happens. If you aren't in compliance they will commiserate but they won't help you.

Security processes for the world outside your business need to be set up but you also consider these suggestions.

Create a list of applications, software, file storage folders and applications you need folks to be locked out on when they leave the business. Then verify they no longer have access.

Ask developers if they have hidden passwords or keys within the application to assist in testing. If they have, make sure they are removed.

- Create a business protocol that defines how passwords should be stored. I know I am sometimes guilty of putting a Post-it note on my computer when I first use a new software product. We all know this is stupid, but I can't tell you how many dozens of passwords I have to remember and use on a weekly basis. It's almost to the point I hate to purchase software because there's another username and password I need to deal with.
- Some developers store their passwords on outside sources lists. This is not a good idea.
- Make sure user access lists stay within the network of the organization. If you ask a vendor to create reports to demonstrate who has access to ensure people have been properly inactivated, keep this data behind the firewall or within your network. Don't email this information and don't put it into a document that could be released in any way. This data is an invitation to a hacker.
- Make sure equipment is returned and confidential data, code or proprietary property returned.
- At least once a year review all access vs. locked down procedures to ensure you have not left something off the list.
- Someone on staff should be given the job of researching security, reviewing procedures and then training staff. For example, anyone on a shared business network should be careful about opening files from an unverified source. Use an email spam collector, junk mail and clutter. I hate clutter because it is too protective; however, I saw it caught an email for me once I may not have. An email was sent to me that looked like it was from my clients; there was one character off in the email address. I may not have seen it if I just went through my hundreds of emails and clicked down my list. This email had a suspicious attachment, so I quickly deleted my entire clutter list to

make sure the email was gone. So take the luck out of making sure you don't open a bad email by using spam filters. Training your staff to know what to watch for is a good idea. Reminding them once a year about security protocol procedures also is a good idea.

- Lastly, make sure you have backups of your data. This includes all business files.

Data isolation

Core data should only be on a server behind a firewall and not on a shared server where you collect random or necessary files. Shared files and information should be set on a separate location, where they are opened and scanned for virus protection. You may have to create processes when a file is opened, the raw data inside the file is copied and entered into either an image or text format free of any code in the original file.

NOTE: It is a mistake to put antivirus on your database server. Whenever the database files change, the antivirus sees the file change and examines it. When database files are in the gigabytes, and every change triggers the antivirus, you get performance hits in the database response time and on the disks.

The old days of looking at a network and seeing everyone's computer including the core data server are gone. The new standards are the core data servers should not be accessible by an open connection. There should be need for login processes to access your core data system. There should be process and personnel limitations as to who can access your core data systems.

Lastly, make sure your personal or business desktop/laptop is protected. Keep updated virus protection on your personal computer, particularly if you use it for emailing or other file sharing products. You also can back up your personal or work PC all the way down to the applications you use. Make sure you keep a series of backups as the latest one could have been corrupted before you knew the virus existed. If you protect your own workspace then you won't run a lower risk of poisoning your work and friends.

Case Summary

A key person of a small company opened an email. The email opened a window that said, "You have been to an illegal illicit site. We will report your activity to the FBI if you do not pay us." The computer was locked down. He couldn't get to his files nor his pictures. Fortunately, he had not emailed anyone nor shared files so the infection stayed on his own device. The worst part of the story is he paid the ransom, but they did not share the key to unencrypt files and release his computer. They just disappeared with the money. Luckily, by uninstalling and reinstalling the operating system, the computer was recoverable and files were backed up so he was able to work again. The ransomware folks are all about payment. They don't care about customer service.

There is an industry around ransomware. There are RAAS (Ransomware as a Service} providers who will attack based upon targets a third-party request them to attack when business is booming. They don't care who they attack; there are no initial or favorite targets. They just look for a demographic that may be willing to pay, like novice computer users or companies where data is their lifeline. They also like to target public sites for notoriety to establish credibility that will resonate fear with subsequent novice targets.

Summary

Review security processes and procedures. When starting new projects make sure security requirements, including roles and data access limitations, are discussed with user, management team and developers. Then, ensure data can be protected from all angles.

Review security processes at least once a year. You may want to hire an outside source to review security and if you believe necessary, hire a professional hacker to look for holes in your systems.

Security is not limited to firewalls and SSL certificates. You need to review internal access procedures, password assignments and management of access of users. Are inactive users locked out of the entire environment? Importantly, make sure there are policies and procedures to lock out developers, DBAs (database administrator) and security engineers to ensure they do not have a way into your environments.

Your computer is not the only device that can be a victim of an attack; phones, hand-held devices and smart watches also are potential targets. The virus once attacking you spreads through your contacts. The attack occurs through disguised websites and applications similar to useful or popular sites and applications. When you click to open the application or site, the virus launches. The application generally cannot be removed through normal means but instead you must use the factory settings to remove the virus. Unfortunately, some viruses control the screen access which does not allow you to get to the settings reset. There are shortcuts for some devices you can use to reset to factory settings without using the screen. Sometimes this works through some other manipulations but often the device is rendered useless.

If you work in a secure environment, private vs. work devices could be a must. Downloading applications to a work device should be held to a minimum, making sure you are only accessing necessary and well-known applications.

Chapter 7

Cloud Environment Security vs. On Premise Environment Security

People are under the assumption that if your data is in a third-party cloud, the data is safe and being taken care of. They say, "I don't have to worry about my data, it is in the cloud." Then cross the room to another group of people who say, "I can't have my data in the cloud; it is too important and the cloud isn't as safe as my own on premises environment."

In actuality, both opinions are incorrect. Cloud environments are not inherently riskier than on premises environments nor are they more secure. Cloud environments have the same security risks as on premises. They all need the same protections and setup demands on the application and cloud environment side.

Statistically, for some reason cloud environments are attacked less often than on premises. I am not sure why this is. Perhaps hackers feel the security is stronger and are less interested in attempting to penetrate it. However, cloud environments are susceptible to Denial of Service (DOS) attacks. This is where one server sends a crushing number of requests to another, basically tying up the attacked server with insignificant queries, overwhelming its ability to do work it was intended for.

Most cloud vendors have sophisticated, and well educated and equipped, security professionals who can adapt to changing security needs. Hiring a team like this for your own environment is costly. But that and all maintenance and support needed by different tiers of the environment can provide comfort to a business owner as cloud fees may be less expensive than having experts on payroll.

The business owner/IT manager or application manager should sit down with the cloud provider and discuss in detail what level of security is on hand. What responsibilities did you hire the cloud provider to take care of? What do they expect to be your responsibilities? You could find holes in these areas.

For example, if your contract doesn't specifically say it covers or watches for DDOs (Distributed Denial of Service) attacks and there is an attack that has filtered through an application, you could incur fees until they are stopped.

Make sure data is being backed up and sent to another site by the cloud provider. Backups on premises (or often on the same server!) are not good at all; you want a backup sent off that site. What if the co-location was under threat of fire or hurricane? You would want data to be offsite so you could quickly get running again. However, these backup processes can be very pricey as the throughput charges from the vendor can be excessive. The best option of making sure you have a copy of your own data may be out of your budget should you store your production environment in a cloud.

If your business requires customers have access to applications or data, you should have a replicated environment on a second cloud environment. These services are offered; it is up to you to take advantage of them.

When you sit down with your provider bring a checklist.

1. Where are my backups?
2. How often are they taken?
3. Where are they kept? (And how do I restore one?)
4. What is your strategy against a DDOS attack?
5. Let's review security processes and yours; are there holes?
   a. Environment access limited?
   b. Data access limited?

    c.   Are checks completed regularly to make sure deactivated accounts are deactivated properly?

    d.   Are you using proper SSL certificates?

    e.   Are developers hiding passwords inside your code?

    f.   Are you sharing passwords in the office?

    g.   Are passwords properly stored and utilized?

    h.   Are firewalls and antivirus software in use on all computers?

    i.   Do you use proper network standards?

    j.   No two computers should share files on the network. The core data structure or database server should not allow other computers to have open access to it

Summary

Security and maintenance strategies need to be applied whether your data is in the cloud or in an on premises environment. Do not assume either environment is safely maintained. Make sure you know, understand and have plans documented> Validate responsibility and document maintenance completion and security plan tasks every single time they occur. You can use a tool to validate your backups, maintenance jobs and security access controls. You should consider a tool so you know every day, hour or minute your environment is protected.

Before moving to the cloud review the costs of proper backup procedures and the cost of the throughput for your users in the application. There may be costs that you had not expected. The costs may still be less than maintaining the hardware, software and staff that you would need on premise but the fact is you still need to know where your data is and in the event of something unforeseen you will need to make sure you can always recover.

It is perhaps no longer an exaggeration to say Internet is everywhere. The corollary to this statement is if your data is accessible with the Internet, usually via a web page, you can get your data from anywhere.

Make sure the database server is behind a firewall, and only the applications accessing the data have means to query the data. When you can, you should use table or column-level data encryption. Limit access to the database except through queries in the application.

Do not under any circumstances allow the data to be accessed directly without using a virtual private network (VPN).

Enforce password complexity standards. Use all the security techniques you can without limiting your performance, use three strike methods to keep bad folks out.

Chapter 8

Why is Database Architecture So Important?

Database architecture focuses on design, maintenance and administration of the software that manages the actual data underlying your application. Correct architecture decisions will have a positive effect on database performance, as well as your ability to scale up.

Maintenance plan/ Manage your data

A certain database management system vendor, a few years back, paid for a Super Bowl commercial where a balloon floated around in a server room, while a party went on in the next room. Forget for a moment once the balloon loses a bit of air, it will likely get sucked into a fan's intake and cause cooling problems with the server. This marketing is the single biggest disservice a vendor has ever performed because every system needs maintenance.

In the same manner, you wouldn't drive your car for too long without a tune up, you can't let your DBMS run without preventive maintenance. And, like an inexpensive commuter car vs. an Italian sportster, the harder and faster your DBMS must run, the more important it is to make sure servers are maintained.

In addition, if databases aren't maintained, you can expect intermittent, followed by snowballing, database performance problems. This is a frequent effect of allowing inexperienced database administrators (as well as network administrators or developers who don't understand database administration) to take care of your systems.

At a minimum, you need to:

1.) Make sure backups are running and are being transferred off site, and a restore is tested periodically. This makes sure in case of a disaster, you have a way to get back to a specific point in time. This includes monitoring database transaction logs to make sure they don't grow unnecessarily.

Regardless of what your technical people tell you, decisions about retention are business, not technical, decisions and generally driven by regulatory reasons. In general, you want to push requirements upon them, not the other way around. If you don't test the restore capability, you don't know if you are really backed up

1. When you are deciding to back up data consider staging backups. One backup a month should be for data that is historical, isn't touched by a lot of users nor can be lost and replaced quickly.

Data that is integral to your business should be backed up at least daily, with incremental backups set up every 15 minutes or every hour depending on space you have available and performance needs. This is the best way to secure data if it is attacked from outside.

If you are a victim of a ransomware attack these backups can be used to bring back your data. If you have staged data and the attack hit last night just before the backup ran, then last night's backup will be bad and unusable. But if you have prior night's backup then you will lose only one days' worth of data, which in most cases causes angst but your business should be able to recover. If you cannot lose one day's worth of data, then you must ensure you are back up and possibly replicating your systems with a warm standby that mirrors applications, code, security and data access of the original server so you can restore to the warm standby.

2. Validate consistency of database

   Apologies for industry jargon – it means you validate absence of corruption in your data indexes and catalogs. This should be performed before backups are aged out.

Rebuild Indexes

Indexes are critical path to performance. Over time, as data changes and grows, indexes become unbalanced in variety of ways. Rebalancing (rebuilding/reorganizing) your index structures has impact on performance.

Update statistics

Modern DBMS have cost-based optimizers. In plain English, when you request information from the database, the DBMS decides the most efficient way of retrieving the data, based upon a histogram it keeps on distribution of data. In a nutshell, when the histogram gets out of date, the approach the server takes to retrieving your data becomes erratic at best.

If you are not certain this work is being performed, it's time to call a consultant.

If I have a properly architected and secure data portal, how can I create gold from my data?

Summary

There are specific data management jobs that need to be run. The jobs themselves are slightly different between database types but they all have one thing in common. The maintenance jobs need to run, they have to be successful in completing their work and should be able to report back details to the IT or management team to provide insight into the environment. Also the jobs should be verifiable and successes and failures should be documented for someone to be able to review the jobs information and determine if action is needed.

Many DBAs and IT managers use scripts that send emails to them to get information, verifying the success of jobs or sending alerts for job failures or when a job itself finds alerting factors. There are tools that can monitor these scripts and show you in simple fashion a quick look into health of your environment. If you are using the script to email tracking system, we suggest looking into a tool that can provide environment health information faster and provide analysis that's easier to understand.

Chapter 9

Prioritizing Environment Workload

If this is the first time you have set up a maintenance schedule and management processes for a technical environment, you may feel overwhelmed. You may be trying to figure out where to start. This may be easy math for you but just in case we thought we would share how to begin the process of evaluating importance of your data, environment and servers.

First, create a list of what you consider to be environments that contain core data.

What data is crucial to keeping your business up and running daily?

What databases run reports critical to cash flow?

What databases or data needs to be backed up, secured, and follow government regulations and auditing processes?

These are environments where you need to start setting up your maintenance and management plans. Typically, these are databases stored on production servers. But as you verify this is true, every so often as a business grows decisions might be made early on that place some development databases on a production server so you will want to be precise when you analyze environments.

If some production environments have replicated, failover, mirrored servers or warm standbys, you may want to set up the maintenance plans in advance for these servers so they can be quickly turned on when or if they get called into action.

After you have production, cash producing, and audited environments set up and maintained, you can then focus on creating maintenance plans for your test, development and support environments.

Our mantra is BACKUP YOUR DATA AND CODE! If you are storing code, methodologies, or need to be able to get back any system to the moment before a crash you should create a backup and maintenance schedule for that environment, especially if you haven't cleaned house. Until you have completed your spring cleaning you may not realize when the production environment ran out of space last year, the IT and business team decided to use a drive on the development server for backups or for general storage. So our advice is back up and maintain all environments. If your developers are using scrum methodologies for application releases and updates, you want to watch those development servers because if you are using scrum your users are expecting rollups to fix issues quickly. Otherwise, a lost development server can cost time and money. Therefore, at least back up the development servers daily and do integrity checks to make sure nothing has become corrupted. [#18F]

If there are inactive development servers, back them up at least so your code is saved.

You often will find backing up development servers is as important as backing up your production servers; losing a development server can mean losing months of work, times dozens of developers.

Summary

Data that affects your bottom line is priority. From there review, discuss and create processes and procedures for other data environments. The reality of how each environment supports your business and job will dictate the amount you spend managing and maintaining that data.

Case Summaries

Case studies here are almost too easy. You can't talk to anybody in the IT industry without hearing stories about data becoming corrupt because of issues with poor care.

Two recent cases:

Many of our customers have come from partner referrals. One recently came because a database became corrupted. Once they identified the corruption, they went looking for backups, and found the backups also had been corrupt. This company had furloughed 1,200 of their 1,400 employees and was getting ready to shut down operations before we came in and were able to mine data from the corrupted database.

In another case, we on-boarded 120 servers for a customer, and as part of the process of validating databases found three corrupted databases, which were returning bad data unknown to application users. We cleaned these up but it should never have gotten to this stage.

At a recent health check, as a small part of the performance work, we were asked to take a few minutes to look at a system which was being used by 3,000 customer service representatives who were downloading 30 days of scheduling data each evening. It was taking more than 30 minutes and getting longer, and the handheld Internet connectivity was timing out in many cases, requiring a restart. With minor index changes, we were able to take down the performance to under 2 minutes, saving 1,500 man-hours each night. The only downside was the 3,000 calls they got that evening asking if something was wrong or whether it was fixed. They told us it was the best 3,000-call night of all time.

I believe as we move about in our daily work activities we sometimes forget to slow down and look at data.

Chapter 10

Creating Your Vault

You have two decisions on where to create your vault, on premises or in the cloud

For pricing consider these costs:

There are hardware and software, operating software, database software and application software costs that need to be evaluated. Teams needed to maintain hardware and software.

And then there's housing for the hardware, environmental costs, cooling and space.

If your data is regulated and if it has actual end owners, then you may want to shelter expenses and create an on premises storage. This can be costly in that you will have hardware maintenance and software maintenance people to employ. The security needs of the data should be your first consideration.

Then move to accessibility; accessibility should not be an issue for either system. Your database and application architecture should be able to handle accessibility and speed issues that are not handled via throughput allowances. This is where you could see a variance in billing that may have you considering an on premises solution. Cloud-based solutions have a high sticker price for I/O. However it may be less than hiring a team to take care of the environment on premises.

If a startup, then the cloud is the place to begin. You have a virtual team making sure the hardware environment is secure and maintained.

This does not mean the software environment will be secure and maintained. Don't assume data is secure and maintained unless it is specifically spelled out in your cloud providers contract.

Your cloud provider may charge extra fees for setting up and storing backups. They also may charge a fee for any performance investigations you need completed for databases. Don't assume you have enough space reserved in your database, either. If you are using Microsoft SQL Server Autogrow then you don't have to watch capacity as tightly but if you are using Sybase ASE or Oracle you may need to watch the database growth yourself, then ask for more space as the database grows.

To encrypt or not to encrypt, that is the question.

Data that is sent out to the universe or sent back should be encrypted. Encrypting the entire database means a lengthier time to upgrade and software upgrades than you may have. You have to basically decrypt the database, send up the data, and then encrypt it again. Check out the encryption section; in short, if you are encrypting everything, make sure you have plenty of CPU on top of processing to deal with encryption/decryption.

Basically, when deciding where to set up the vault your budget will probably be the factor in that decision.

Chapter 11

HIPAA, SOC, and PCI Compliance

It almost seems like the government is trying to put more regulatory restrictions on data than it knows we can handle.

We have one client, a quasi-government agency with financial requirements, with 12 mandatory audits per year. The agency has built entire systems around being able to provide data to auditors. If regulatory agencies are trying to handcuff us with busy work, causing companies to spend shareholder money on reporting, they are succeeding.

Compliance for these, and all other, regulations begins with creating and putting in place standards, processes and user training. Note recurring user training, while pretty much stupid, patronizing, and insulting, is generally mandated by regulation.

Let's first discuss access.

In our company and most of our client's companies, nobody has access to a data-rich environment without proper background check. I am not certain this is a step that will protect us but it makes us feel better and I believe it sets expectations for integrity from the first moment of hiring someone.

Then we provide access: If this person is a user or a DBA you should consider limiting access through roles, passwords and log-ins.

When someone is no longer responsible for that work, or moves on in life, make sure the person is locked out of all systems, and then immediately verify the lockout. Don't wait for the quarterly user access reports; verify now. Just in case, this is good business practice that will help make management happy with your processes.

Next, ensure you have firewalls, and virus protection not only installed but regularly updated because there are reactions that need to be adjusted as hackers become more effective.

Now let's talk about compliance. HIPAA is one of the more onerous sets of regulations. Here's an excerpt from a HIPAA requirements <u>checklist</u>. [#11]

There are three parts to the HIPAA Security Rule – technical, physical and administrative safeguards – and we will address each of these in order in our HIPAA compliance checklist.

Keep the personal data safe

Keep the ePHI (electronic personal health information, sometimes just PHI) data safe by using the technological advances available. The ePHI or PI (personal information) must be protected while allowing the owner to have access to the data. While at rest or being transported the data must be encrypted to the NIST standards (National Institute of Standards). Data ePHI data that travels outside the firewalls the data must be encrypted and the receiver needs to have their own processes and protocols to protect the data. This is so any breach of confidential patient data renders the data unreadable, undecipherable and unusable.

Limit access control: This not only means creating and assigning user names, PINs and other access limitations but also to create procedures to properly govern disclosure or release of information during an emergency.

Determining access and long-term storage of ePHI:

While planning for short and long-term storage of personal information, you must consider the proper mechanisms for collecting and keeping the information, safe, refer to the regulations for how long the information needs to be kept and readily accessible to the PI information owner. Storing the data can be very expensive.

Encrypt and decrypt the data: The PI information must be encrypted but must also be able to be decrypted and available to all parties that have the legal permissions of the PI owner. Therefore, the data not only has to be stored and protected but also readily accessible.

Set up audit and proper reporting: You must ensure that not only that the data is protected but if unauthorized users or outside attacks have occurred you must create auditing and reporting processes to review, record and report the occurrence. Monthly or quarterly reviews should be set up and shared between the IT team and business management.

Ensure that you have automated log of: You must create a timed out log off procedure should data access be left open by a user. There should be a mechanism to close out the application and stop the viewing or transmitting of the data on the user's computer.

Protect the physical environment: The physical environment where the data resides must have security processes. If the access is in a data center, cloud center, or on-premise limitations to personnel and mobile devices in the vicinity need to be limited, tracked and audited.

Facility or premise access: You must set up on-premise personnel access procedures for any persons that have access to the building or infrastructure. This includes but is not limited to software engineers, hardware engineers, vendors, contractors and building maintenance people. The procedures also must include safeguards to prevent unauthorized access, tampering and theft. The management team should train and revisit the rules for the facility access with employees and review the procedures for best practices.

Workstation policies, access and viewing: Workstations are the window to the data therefore policies must be put into place to make sure workstations are not left on and connected to the applications with the ePHI. Access to each work station should be limited to specific users in a highly data rich environment. Screens should not be viewable by non-authorized personnel so that should not be in the line of sight of the general population in the room or office. From time to time you should check to make sure that only active personnel have access to the workstation that there are no shared user names or passwords and revisit your sign on and activation and deactivation procedures in the work environment

Mobile device procedures : If mobile devices such as phones or tablets are used, then proper procedures for access to the devices, secure lock up when not in use and data removal from the devices is mandatory even if devices are deactivated and sent to be destroyed.

Inventory of hardware (addressable): Inventory of all hardware and data storage must be maintained. Migrated data must be accessible for the owner of the ePHI.

Mobile device procedures Personnel Administrative Safeguards are policies and procedures that bring together the Privacy Rule and the Security Rule. They are the pivotal elements of a HIPAA compliance checklist and require a security officer and privacy officer be assigned to put measures in place to protect ePHI, while they also govern conduct of the workforce. This officer should work with IT Managers and line of business managers to ensure that protocols that are in place are followed during daily work activity.

The OCR (Optical Character Recognition) pilot audits identified risk assessments as the major area of Security Rule non-compliance. Risk assessments are going to be checked thoroughly in the second phase of the audits; not just to make sure the organization has conducted one, but to ensure they are comprehensive and ongoing. A risk assessment is not a one-time requirement, but a periodic task necessary to ensure continued compliance. The administrative safeguards include:

> **Risk assessments must be prepared:** Security officers, IT departments and line of business owners need to prepare, set up and stage risk assessments to ensure that all ePHI is protected throughout the life of the data within the corporation.

Create a risk assessment policy and procedures protocol: A risk assessment plan must be implemented where policies and procedures are tested. This should include all employees with access to the ePHI data and if they are not working within the compliance of your standards they need to be retrained. These assessments should be regularly scheduled. This assessment may include outside vendors who have access or may also be transmitting the ePHI data.

Set up training standards: Training sessions should be scheduled regularly and should include malware and proper documentation handling within and outside the corporate fire walls.

Disaster recovery plans: In the event of an emergency, no matter if it is weather, manmade or hardware related a plan for protecting and providing access to the ePHI data is necessary.

Testing the disaster recovery plans: The disaster recovery plan needs to be tested and verified. The data must be restorable and hardware and software must be in place in order to allow for access to the ePHI.

Third party/subcontractor and vendor access restrictions: The security officer, IT and line of business owners need to be mindful of and restrict access to the ePHI data. The vendors, subcontractors and others need to have training. Review proper protocols with all third-party personnel. These procedures should be tested and reviewed within the same schedules as the other data process audits within your organization. All parties should be required to be trained, follow procedures and should also be told to share any misconduct, errors or breaches that may arise during their service.

Data breaches: If a data breach occurs then processes for reporting must be in place. These processes should be shared with all employees. As all other processes, these protocols should be tested and reviewed from time to time.

Summary

Many industries have onerous, mandatory reporting requirements for government agencies. If you are in, or starting, a business with data requirements that might include personal health care information, credit or credit card information, be sure you either have compliance knowledge, or can rent it, meaning find somebody who does.

Note this is specialized and not something to guess at. In this summary, we have provided a checklist to help guide you through the mandatory HIPAA, SOC and PCI regulations. This list might help you navigate through tasks you need to think through along with information from the <u>website</u>. [#10F]

This might be the time to help you create a to-do list.

1. Ask, "How important your data is to your business?"
    a. Do you have PI (Personal Information) that is "owned" by someone else?
    b. Do you have regulations or other reporting mandated?
    c. Do you have vendors or subcontractors that need to be trained?
2. Can you afford to lose any amount of data?
3. How fast can you re-establish lost data?
4. How fast do you need recovery to be?
5. Do you have a disaster recovery plan?
    a. Do you have audits and internal disaster recovery testing regularly scheduled?
    b. If no, start listing your critical environment platforms
        i.   Hardware
        ii.   Software
        iii. Applications
        iv.   Security and firewall redundancies
    c. Which applications that are crucial to keeping your business running

        i.   Client portals?

        ii. Regulated Reporting Services?

        iii. Billing, or inventory or other basic business support systems?

  d. Hardware that runs them

  e. Software that runs them

  f. How fast can you get the environment reinstalled and running?

  g. Have you considered using some type of replication or High Availability in order to prevent costs while you are waiting for systems to be restored?

6. What data is vital?

  a. Client data?

  b. Regulated data?

        i.   Are crucial databases backed up

        ii. Are crucial databases restorable?

        iii. Is this data leaving your environment, through emails, application access, or any other way? Then consider encrypting it

7. Access Issues

  a. What are your security protocols?

  b. Do you have a security access protocol designed, put in place and tested?

  c. Are they verified?

        1. Do you verify people have proper access?

        2. Do you verify people don't share access information?

        3. Do you verify once people are inactivated is their access restricted properly?

  d. Are all people trained to follow the security protocols?

  e. Ask your technologists if encryption is needed for data transfer

8. Data usefulness

  a. Do you have data that is no longer vital on vital systems?

b. Do you have data that could be data warehoused so you can help improve performance and relieve some of the data management money you use to protect the data?

c. Do you have applications, software or data that is no longer useful and can be archived or officially trashed, creating room for growth?

If you cannot answer any of these questions, take this list to your IT staff. If there are holes, check with your IT staff and fill them in.

Chapter 12

How is data manipulated?

Do you remember commercials that said 4 of 5 dentists surveyed found Crest/Colgate toothpaste the best? Or the campaign that said 9 of 10 doctors prescribed Advil?

It is sometimes phrased as "nine of *these* 10 doctors agree," showing you a group of men in white coats with stethoscopes; this is a clue to what's really going on.

Your brain hears "nine of 10 doctors agree" and reads it as "90 percent of doctors agree." But that's not necessarily what happened. The sample size and population can be anything the advertiser wants, including having a panel of only 10 doctors asked and cherry picking doctors until they get the result they want.

Alternatively, the claim may reflect reality, but what is being claimed isn't the same as what is being sold. Listen carefully. Did 9 of 10 dentists really say their brand of toothpaste was best, or did 9 of 10 dentists just agree *toothpaste in general* is a good idea? Did they say they would recommend *this* brand over all other brands, or did they just say they would recommend it? [#12F]

Sometimes in our reporting we must continually re-evaluate data we are collecting.

For example, we run reports that let us know how much time we are working for each of our clients. It turns out our people use the software we created differently than we had initially thought out with Use Cases. This means we would run a query that said how much time this person worked overall. Then we would run reports by clients and projects. Guess what? The totals didn't match. We had to go back to find out why. It turned out when creating one report, we had rules and expectations to ensure we did not double bill hours. Other rules ensured work that overran between months only was accounted for in the month those hours were worked. This made it difficult to go back and run another report by user and validate the work effort all around. Eventually we identified all rules that were put in place for each report and, where necessary, we made sure rules were the same for each report but allowing the diversity needed for the user. Now we have accurate reports we can verify. In reporting, this seems to be a constant issue.

We believe if we ask a question of our systems, we will get direct answers. But sometimes our thoughtfulness during other report creation to validate the data interferes with another report or at least interrupts the ability to validate data.

So there are red states vs. blue states, wealthy vs. poor, educated vs. the uneducated. In the end we are all data hoarders. We collect baseball and football statistics. We watch election polls. We watch data that is shared by the American Medical Associations and others. We research whether our kids should be vaccinated, sleep on their backs, eat eggs and bacon, or whole grains and fruit. Tequila is a miracle drink and marijuana is healthy with no long-term side-effects and a cure for diseases.

The truth is data matters. It has value; it is sought after.

We read, listen, watch folks share, interpret and misinterpret data to evoke responses from others.

How to check the accuracy of data

Is my data accurate? How can I tell if my reports are bringing back all correct information? How do I verify results I am getting so I know what I am sending out in reports is correct?

The first step is to review architecture of your data. Refer back to Chapter 8, "Why is the Database Architecture So Important?"

Many times, I run reports out of our system and I know something is missing. The data is not quite correct. In the end, it is usually because I am not asking the question I believed I was asking. For example, sometimes date ranges include insert or update dates but not end dates when running a query by date range. Or sometimes I have not included all proper parameters or I specified too many and cleared out a host of results because my own vision was too narrow. Other times I realize the report is wrong and I just found a bug I need to send on up to development.

There are ways I can check my own data against itself. Other times, I will need to ask the DBA to help run the query to see if the data set is same as mine in the application. This helps me find bugs in my report and the way I have set up the query for myself.

1. Verify if the query or request you created is bringing you back the general information you wanted. Are the data types, date ranges and specifications correct? Is there a full accounting of the dates? Does the data fall in line with date range or is something off?
2. Look to see if the number of rows being returned makes sense,
3. Check for duplicates. If there are no duplicates, check to see if rows are blank.
4. Test data as you add or take away parameters; does the data make sense?
5. Lastly, randomly pick data and verify its authenticity in other reports.

If you want to run a data integrity check then run a similar report with other parameters on the live data to see if, between the two reports, there are omissions or duplicates that should exist in both reports.

Testing accuracy of data in reports should be done during the quality assurance phase of development. I have the DBAs run the same query in the code and I run the report on the application side and we review to see if they show the correct data set. If they match parameter to parameter and row to row, I am fairly certain we have just created a useful report that will show the data correctly, accurately and I will have confidence in reports sent to clients. Each time we adjust the reports, add new parameters or add new reporting features, we have to carefully test all the data and reports affiliated with the same data. Believe it or not during testing phases we often find the question I believed I was asking wasn't always the query they wrote for me. Sometimes definitions, date usage expectations and poorly written specifications show up at this point. We go back to the drawing board and work on the query. It is more fun to do this now and less stressful than running a report that needs to be sent out to another party when you realize data is missing, or there is duplicate or poor data in your report. Puzzles are fun to solve without a time clock.

Quality assurance testing

Don't ever forget this step during any rollup. Just like a jeweler will use the eye loupe to make sure gems are real, use a discerning eye to review any code that is going to be rolled up to your application, database, database code, stored procedures, table changes or index changes.

We all have tested code sent to deploy to production. When we deploy IT the code caused all kinds of heck with the systems. The size nor the importance of the data or the rollout seems to assuage folks from rolling up without fully testing the code. Some folks believe if they run an error check on the code that is enough. Or if they run the code and the result on the single page or application process, the test is complete.

I have been hit by this bug a couple of times. I believe I have a simple application change. Expecting the change to affect only one screen or process, and then we roll up and boy do I look dumb! All of a sudden I am getting calls from users saying. "I found these bugs after this morning's rollup." This is all because I assumed I was correct and this was a simple change that shouldn't affect anyone's work but my own. Never assume. Always review application, always take all users perspective into consideration and above all else test before you roll it up to production. The worst thing that happens is you delay a bad rollup from happening and save people from pain.

SCRUM application design processes are fabulous. We follow the SCRUM processes. It seems while trying to meet these fast-paced goals, we all do what SCRUM did not intend and that is to mitigate or take for granted the value of developing testing procedures and sticking with those procedures. I believe the date for the rollup tends to take precedence over the value of testing and proper quality assurance. This was never the intention of the authors of SCRUM, Agile. If you look at their documentation under the section "Define Done," they state each increment should be thoroughly tested. I have not read anything in their manual that said unless your deadline is fast approaching, then go ahead and skip testing.

Testing applications and code before a rollup is one of the stepping stones to protect your asset. If you roll up a large application change that changes your data control strategies or infiltrates the way data is stored, viewed, saved and updated, you may be able to roll back the code but it is possible you will have a heck of a time changing the effects on the data itself.

So if you insist on rolling up without proper testing, I would test your ability to properly restore from a backup because you may be doing this in the middle of the night right before your most important reports are running. This is a bad day for everybody.

Case Summary

Garbage in garbage out. I am not trying to be political, but a famous case for poor data collection, data analysis and activities created by data, was reason for going into Iraq. On the ground there were sightings, satellite pictures, verbal communications and prior acts of use and yet when we went into Iraq there were no weapons of mass destruction. We could not find them after we had basically overrun the country.

Now some assume the data was falsified to validate the start of a war; others believed they may have been destroyed or relocated before we found them. Still others believe it existed but not to the amount predicted, or these weapons were taken into Syria by truck before we got there. Now over a decade later biological weapons were used against Syria's own people. Is this a coincidence or did we miss the boat? Were we too late in collecting the data and activating results? Did the data ever exist? Did we react incorrectly to the data we analyzed; maybe the weapons were in another country all along?

If we cannot verify data with any degree of accuracy, if we cannot ask the right questions, if we assume answers, then we will not be able to react, and create a response that will help us keep customers. We will push them away to our competitors, never to regain trust.

Summary

In any project, you need to set up standards. The standards must include testing processes and procedures and validation of the testing itself. Sometimes we think just creating a test plan is enough, but is the test plan valid? Did you think of all pitfalls you may encounter? Did you create Use Cases that may not be inherently recognized but include processes relative to this process with rules that are changed or affected? Rolling up using Agile Thought's Scrum processes doesn't mean you skip the testing and quality assurance phase. It just means you are taking bite-sized pieces of a project so you can roll up and test faster.

You must remember to test everything, the failures along with the successes. Sometimes failures are harder to test but they are vital in a successful rollout. For example, you may test to make sure the user name and password insert in a log-in works, but you also need to test a bad user name and password to make sure a person cannot get in. These seem simple but using this scenario provides the importance of failure testing.

Also, don't forget to make sure inner pages on your web application are not opening when a person just enters or clicks on an old link; make sure if they are not logged in the page brings them to the log-in page. If you change anything to do with logging in roles, code, stored procedures, tables and encryption, test it all again. Then use this methodology for all other testing. Anything related must be tested. We try to test everything all over again when we roll up because it is difficult after using and building a project, to review, remember and create a test plan based upon assumed relationships.

While writing this book we saw a story on TV and online that discusses the problems of fake news and fake news creators. This information highlights the need to always check and double check data and the information you are gathering. The sources, the reports and the authors need to all have credibility checks. In 2016, 62 percent of the U.S adult population use social media as the news source. Many of those news stores are fake. There is a group of fake news developers on the internet whose job is to create stories that look real, providing unverifiable sources and facts while working together to push the stories into social media. Many of those stories are being picked up by credible news journalists and ruining their reputations for not doing fact-finding due diligence. Facebook, for example, is working on creating processes to verify or mark stories as unverifiable and to weed out fake news. Russia used fake news stories in social media to push their own agenda in our election and tried to do the same thing to interfere with France's election but their process was discovered. It is interesting how information and our data collections can be manipulated in treacherous ways. As society develops ways to tie us together, we will build great databases of knowledge that will help us but someone will always try to manipulate it for their own agenda, An example of good data is the National Integrated Ballistic Information Database. This database holds ballistic information for old and new cases. Bullet markings can be compared between cases. Old cases are being resurrected through new case investigations and both cases are closing as forensic evidence lines up in both cases. The ballistic information creates new relationships between facts in different cases and uses real data to solve those cases. Social media is finding new ways to stop fake news from infecting our daily lives. Both require extensive maintenance and evaluation; both will affect our society in ways we may not understand to this date.

Chapter 13

How to Turn Data into Gold

If you don't believe you can turn data into gold then Google how to turn data into cash and see how many articles have been written in Forbes and other magazines.

Forbes says not only should you consider it but you are leaving money on the table if not. The magazine also says if you aren't doing the right thing with data you can bet your competitors are.

Through my research, I see there are a couple of ways to turn data into cash.

The first way is to look at data and metadata to see if there is value in selling that data.

The second way is to analyze data and metadata you have to show trends you can evaluate. You can become knowledgeable about customers and competitors to create marketing campaigns, new products or services, or improve a relationship with clients.

In either of these methods to find hardcore monetized value in data, you must first review and cleanse the data. Also, you want to be sure you have kept enough data to show trends and enlighten the audience. In other chapters in this book I mentioned you want to be sure you clean up data and make room for data you need. In this chapter, we will be saying make sure you keep everything you will need to create value for this process.

This is a bit contradictory, but in reality, it's all about making sure you keep valuable data and dump anything, not of value. However, you may want to look at data with a new pair of eyes to double check if there is no value, especially in the metadata. The metadata can be surprisingly valuable depending on what you are collecting and how detailed it is. (#13F)

Strategy to use the data you have

The best approach I have read is to glean data and turn it into a viable asset. Find out in an article by David Booth in marketingland.com. (#13AF)

For example, telephone companies track phone calls. During this process they collect the time, how long was the call, the phone numbers, and where you were when each party was on the call. It's the same with texts and other data communications. So what if the telecommunications company was able to distinguish that a number of people are located at certain spots throughout the day, such as near the mall, at train or bus stations, or at traffic stops. This information may help vendors at the mall see when traffic is higher or lower, which bus stops are used most and which train stops are most active. All this information has a different value for different people, but it's all the same data they are collecting.

What if the same data helped the telecommunications company create apps or other access to share with clients who ride the train? Which train stops are busiest at which time of day? Which traffic routes are easier throughout the day, or when someone's favorite store at the mall is having its next sale? Then, the telecommunications company can strengthen the relationship with clients.

As an owner of data, you can choose to use it to create good karma with its customers as a longer-term investment. You can add money to the bottom line by selling this data. Most likely you will consider doing both.

The process of turning the data into cash is making sure you review the data, validate it and look at it from a bird's-eye view. Take off your limited perspective as to how the data can be used and look at it as though you just walked into a room with all this information at your fingertips. Then try to play a symphony.

After you query and research the data, work on the presentation. Are there visual displays you can create from the data that will attract attention and excite your audience?

Can you take the enormous spreadsheets you usually review for your sales meetings and create graphs and visuals that will transform the information into a new vision?

The strategy to employ to make your data valuable

Look at your data from a new perspective

Step back and take a fresh view of the data. What exactly have you been collecting in your system? What information is there you may have overlooked over the years? Don't just look at the same reports you are used to viewing. If necessary, ask the IT staff to send a few rows with column names and metadata information intact to see what is stored vs. what data you are accessing.

Then review this data; look for patterns or stories that have been left out over time. Delve into the past; what has changed? Is there anything that pops out? For example, did you see a once hot item turn cold? Do you see something sells well in some demographics but not others? Is there an item you didn't realize sells well to a particular age group but not others? Dig deep.

If you can, take back this information to your reports and dig through details of the information to re-investigate what reports were showing but you hadn't seen the entire picture because the excitement led you elsewhere.

Open up your mind and don't use the same formulas or preconceptions to guide your journey. Use graphical tools to create compelling images for your mind to sort through. Compare dates, parameters and other values with each other and mine through all aspects of your queries.

Dig into your history

Now drill deep into the past. Look for old vs. new patterns. What is revealed to you? Can you create a story line that will show you insights into what you have seen in the past vs. what is going on now? Can you create new stories such as the telecommunications company, which initially used the data as to when who and where calls originated and connected for billing? Now they can see a broad range of characteristics and client behaviors that are shared through metadata of their information. How often do they call a friend while sitting at Starbucks in the morning getting coffee? How long is the average call? Do the calls tend to end in less than 5-10 minutes and only last until they get their turn in line? Do the calls tend to be with the same people, family, and co-workers? Do cell phone users tend to use the data while sitting in Starbucks? If so, do they use email or are they shopping or using social media?

All these patterns may mean something of value to a vendor, or they may mean more for the telecommunications company. Should the company offer to sell Starbucks coupons to their clients at 6 a.m. for those who frequent Starbucks each day? Should they sell the list to Dunkin' Donuts so the company can try to pick up market share by offering faster, better and less expensive coffee?

Or could the telephone company simply share the fact there are no wait times at Starbucks this morning; you can have a fresh cup soon.

So review your data; do you see something surprising? Maybe there is a segment of your market where people of a certain age like to purchase your merchandise, but they like select colors, sizes or they only shop weeknights or weekdays. You missed the window of opportunity because most brands show the item in white and you never show coupons online at night, or you don't take advantage of advertising that would reach the age group.

Make sure the data has meaning

When you present your story about missed tales of the past be sure, you include information that would help to bring the audience into perspective. For example, if you said you sold X number of blue items to teenagers last month, bring the details into the data. State that you sold X items to particular age groups in specific colors. Show differences in the demographics, then show questions and strategies against your findings, to complete the story. Make sure the summary is sound, clear and concise. Allow your audience to develop its fascination with the story and create own investigations.

Use your data to connect to your target audience

We have mentioned a few ideas on our way through the process. As you are investigating and looking for stories, patterns, and scenarios you also are finding a connection with clients. You are strolling through buying processes as you filter data. You also may review their profiles online and on social media. Or you may filter, like Amazon, for those who purchased this item also purchased these items. If we discovered that your client frequents Starbucks, send them a coupon gift. If they buy a food item in 30 days, offer a BOGO for the same item to bring them back to your brand.

Match the messaging to the demographics; if the person is married with children, offer incentives that may help them enjoy a product with their child or provide escapes without them. If the customers are young and single offer single-serving packets or send them coupons to share with a friend. If the person is retired, offer coupons that will help bring them to your site, store or restaurant when you need to fill seats. Those early birds help keep your team fed and fill in those seats while everyone else is in the middle of the days' end commute. You know how much retirees like those early bird specials.

Engage your audience by using data to define your strategy

As you are enticing more engagement with the client, you are collecting more data about them. Were they willing to fill in the survey? What rewards worked? How long did you keep the brand loyalty? Eventually, you may entice them to be a referral, sending out coupons to share with friends. This data can be used to create platforms and lists for other avenues of reaching out and connecting with them. Creating an invaluable dialogue, you can review again in six months or five years from now to gain insight into the growth of your marketplace.

Use your old data as a crystal ball to predict your future

In your story use the old data, today's stories and scenarios to guess how you can re-animate relationships with customers. Create ideas about what other data you would like to start collecting, what information is vital for growth and how that information may affect the company. Create scenarios that can be evaluated later against your predictions. Make predictions clear enough that you can evaluate later. Try to create scenarios with enough detail you can follow certain demographics to find out if predictions were founded or if the data gave you new light and a new path to take. Let the data lead but let your imagination locate the road.

You may want to follow up with an email or text message that thanks them for their recent purchase. Ask them if they liked the product in a survey offering a coupon for filling out the survey. Most people don't mind polls if they are quick and offer something in return. Invite them to rate you on Facebook, your website in Google or provide a testimonial you can use as a reference.

Case Summary

If you could run reports that align customer wants and needs to the data you track and the messages to your target market, wouldn't that help your bottom line? Facebook and Google are working together to try to predetermine what kind of ads you may want to see. They work together between searches and the likes we choose while online. They are trying to read our minds. This is cool at times and scary at others. Do we want a vendor to know so much about us they can select products we may need before we are aware we want them? However, aren't we looking for ways to ease our lives, so we have more fun time? For example, Staples has the easy button. We can keep the buttons in our laundry rooms, garages, kitchens and push the button. Staples holds the data and knows how much, what brand, where we are and can ship it to our door. We can assume they will use data to investigate future needs of not only purchases but services they can provide later to create a lifetime customer of us all.

Summary

Your data may have value you don't even realize until you step back and review it. You may want to record wish lists to formulate processes that could help you get the information you know is hidden, but you just need to figure out a way to allow the information to be revealed.

There are processes to follow just as there are for any project to be successful. They fall into categories of review, analyze, process and share in exciting ways. Then consider the market to see if there is value in gems you are holding. You may have to look outside the standard playing field; imagination and intelligent review are keys to finding nuggets valuable to someone else. There is a market for data; you have to determine if you want to do the work to find the markets and if you have information worth the effort.

Chapter 14

How Law Enforcement Uses Data

Articles in Popular Mechanics and Fortune surprised us. I did not realize my phone data is not mine. That FBI and other law enforcement agencies are purchasing this data from phone companies and mining it for criminal activity. They don't need warrants and can review data to find details to hunt criminals. [#14F]

We know some employers use Facebook to hire employees, although this trend is beginning to go away. We have seen on TV after a person has committed a heinous act, law enforcement will review social media pages to find clues as to their beliefs, intentions or state of mind. What we didn't realize is there are organizations that track these pages to warn law enforcement about possible acts such as protests. There are organizations paid to create algorithms and other web crawlers to find groups or individuals that may want to disrupt an event, a school or government agencies.

Case Summary

The FBI search data looking for voice, text or emails with certain words that may lead to particular crimes. We accept the intrusion in our private world. If we did not allow intrusion, we would not use these devices.

To be able to use Internet, social media and cell phones, we understand personal data is not entirely our own. For a short while, we believed snap chats were free areas of expression and could not be traced because data was deleted after a short time. It turns out data is removed from individual servers and devices, but the data does not vanish. The data resides on the originating service providers' data environment and therefore can be used against you by law enforcement. Nothing you create that escapes into the world further than your bedroom is private. Privacy only means acts, things, thoughts, ideas, images that are locked up inside your home and not shared with anyone outside it. There is a new era, and it does not mean everything you own is personal.

How law enforcement is using big data

In an article by Doug Wyllie, an editor of <u>Police One</u>, he tells us how Big Data is helping the budgets for crime investigation units with the police force. [14CF]

With shrinking budgets and in some towns a shrinking police force, this relates to how big data is helping law enforcement.

Using large amounts of data is not like what you see in police shows where they can hack into any state and local municipality or business systems to get their guy. On TV the data seems to magically appear, with beautiful pictures and clear data congruencies making it obvious this is the criminal. The searches and analysis are a lot more complicated. The job requires specialists in data collection, scrubbing and then retrieval. After that job, you need a criminal analyst to sift through data, review profiles and connect dots from all data sources. This means the new police department isn't made up of those on the street crime fighters. The tough street guys now need to work with the nerd patrol of civilians to get crimes solved.

Also in this article, Wyllie says service providers such as IBM are creating Intelligent Operation Centers in Smart Cities that join crime analytics with predictive policing. It provides, "A holistic view, of information to help police protect transportation systems, water, utilities, and provide social services."

This data analysis may help police not only protect life and property but to better serve and understand communities and create a more efficient approach to community-wide crime issues. This may contribute to creating a partnership between law enforcement and social service providers so before communities become worn down by criminal activity; municipalities can provide services to help residents with a safety net and improved public relations.

Big data and pre-crime prevention

In an article on wired.com, Yaniv Mor discusses the reality of the "Minority Report." Minority Report was a predictive crime analysis tool which caught criminals before they acted. **(#14DF)**

The author notes we have been pre-determining criminal actions for some time. By searching out terrorist cells, whether homegrown or imported, we have been using data gathering to figure out who is doing what. We look for large buys of certain materials; we look for money transfers in large amounts and from individual organizations; we search on social media, phone and text logs or characters between groups to root out people with criminal intentions.

What you will learn in this article is just how close we are to pre-determining individual criminal acts. Homeland Security has started a project called FAST. Future Attribute Screening Technology Project can identify potential terrorists by using mobile computer labs to monitor individual's vital signs, body language, and other physiological patterns

Rutgers University is creating a crime prevention application that looks at the geography of criminal activities, what type of businesses are in the vicinity, and creates relationships between criminal trends and neighborhoods. With this data, they develop analysis to predict expected criminal activities. I imagine they will eventually include economic patterns, such as jobs losses in the area, weather patterns and holiday and tourist traffic to predict up and down swings of criminal activity. This may help with planning shifts for police and create an effective prevention force.

LexisNexis Risk Solutions, Social Media Monitor, is a SAAS (Software as a Service) that helps to catch bad guys who like to brag. This product allows users to monitor social networking sites for posts, status updates, and profiles. Since many criminals are not intelligent or are just looking for their 15 minutes of fame, many will brag or leave clues before or after they have committed a crime. An officer can commit searches on local social posters to look for clues in private profiles. This data can be used in a court of law.

Social agencies will use this tool as well to track parents of children who were taken into foster care. Sometimes they will use social media to find relatives to help bring together the family. They may find dads who have walked out or use pictures and profiles to analyze whether parents may be able to correct their actions or if they are continuing to abuse drugs or alcohol. People don't think about what they post. They have an illusion of privacy in a public platform, which is curious because we use social media to share thoughts with the world.

An update on crime tracking of U.S citizens.

The NSA changed the rules just recently. The NSA will stop watching citizen's media traffic through warrantless wiretapping and email communications that mention foreign people of interest under Section 702 of the Foreign Intelligence Surveillance Act. **(#14EF)**

This March, Congress approved a bill that will allow internet providers to sell your web browser history. The data that is revealed is not directly personal. Your name, Social Security account or bank information are not shared. Demographics are shared; the fact you are a woman living in particular city or county, with homes sold in a certain price range, and your browser history, all this is shared. This data is personal but not precious, and it has been collected by companies over decades in other less readily transparent ways, such as magazine subscriptions, catalog orders, large purchases and coupons used in stores. We should be used to this, but each time our data is shared we feel a like someone has just stolen a bit more of our soul. **(#14F)**

Summary

In years to come, individuals may hire other organizations to go into the spidery reaches of the web and cleanse their data. We can see the day when a teenager trying to make a living who may have protested a bit too much about a political movement or was involved with a questionable group, will want their data cleansed. We also can imagine a time when the web will be required to clean out data older than 3, 5 or 10 years to be purged just like criminal and credit information is purged after ten years.

As data grows and is used and abused, the opportunity for regulation and new businesses continue to grow. Criminals may one day change the way we use data just because they exist. The more laws are broken, the more laws will be made to "protect" society. How far will the reach go? One day will we all be convinced shutting off technology is the best to preserve our legal rights? Or will the intrusion become expected and we all are resigned to live in a world where leaders guide our will without a whimper from us?

It will be interesting to see how this evolves. Will access to data create a world that is more accepting and reassuring or will it create new microcosms of society that will judge, blame and cause more dissension between people? I can see where we may create online cliques where we only "like" people who have our political point of view, same eye color or same religion. Wouldn't it be nice if the Internet of things creates communities of openness, honesty, and trust so we can share ideas, thoughts and life differences for a better planet? These days with the buildup of outrageous animosity and distrust I am worried but ever hopeful technology will unite us. The powers that are responsible for re-sharing data need to be aware of their responsibilities to ensure the data is valid. The government needs to consider our privacy while allowing businesses to grow through technology and communications.

Chapter 15

In Which Direction is Technology Trending?

Information technology may not have invented buzz words and acronyms, but IT certainly has owned it from a volume perspective.

Also, with an enormous amount of capital, and ability to purchase marketing savvy, IT has been able to push technology into the modern gestalt in a way unheard of even ten years ago. As an example, look at the long lines outside Apple stores every time a new phone comes out. Apple has had staying power, though.

What about technology gaming trends? The digital Pokémon craze, which seemed to sweep the world, didn't last more than a short while.

It becomes necessary, then, to be able to identify which technologies are here for good, and which is going the way of the dinosaurs, and how quickly. Motivations are a great place to start.

Let's start by talking about IT staffing in general.

People in IT are change-adverse. If it hadn't been around, they'd have invented the phrase, "If it ain't broke, don't fix it." In fact, when something goes wrong, the experienced IT staffer's first question is usually, "What changed?"

Sadly, though, software ages and needs to be updated, to resolve bugs as well as to close security holes hackers seem to keep finding. So, we need to balance the following:

1.) Don't be the first person on the block to apply the upgrade; the upgrade itself is a risk, which requires extensive testing. If somebody else finds the bug in the upgrade first, it saves you aggravation.

2.) If you wait too long to apply the upgrade when you need help your software vendor will point and laugh. They'll tell you they can't help because the software is too old, then you're going to have to upgrade in a hurry, rather than in an orderly, careful manner.

When things are running smoothly, IT folks will push back on changes.

That said, IT staff tend to be innovative when they are trying to solve a problem. We've spoken about security — what happens when bureaucrats, in their wisdom, decide data on disks need to be encrypted? (This is not a bad idea and secures data against theft of devices.) Now, options include:

- Encrypt at the application level, with some hashing algorithm – this is unusual today, as there are many options which are less work.
- Encrypt at the DBMS level (that is, make the database do the work) – this has become more common and getting easier. In the past, you could choose to encrypt at the column or database level; today, many DBMS vendors provide full-time data encryption. Note, this requires additional CPU to manage the encryption
- Hardware encryption – defer the problem from the application and database. Instead, allow hardware vendors to handle the extra workload external to the database. Make sure if you choose this route you are selecting a hardware vendor with staying power – that is, one who is established, profitable and has sold more than two storage units.

This is where your IT staff will excel, as they will test every option, weigh pros and cons, and retest.

IT folks love technology. Once decisions are made, though, they want to stay with it.

Now let's talk about IT executives.

While IT executives may ascend through the ranks of organizations, and some are out of MBA-type programs, all IT executives are, in the end, business managers. They are responsible for budgets, projections, resources and ultimate success of the department. As managers, they are looking at the bigger picture. They're not asking "What's the best way to encrypt." Instead, they're asking, "What's the most cost-effective, long-term approach to make sure data is protected and are we in compliance with regulatory agencies and our auditing standard and needs? Can I replicate this approach across my organization so that I can solve the problem only once and apply it to other problems?"

IT executives also are looking to resolve issues from software licensing, hardware maintenance, personnel management, scheduling and training, and other factors unrelated to technology, but related to administration of the technology.

Among them is the longevity of technologies. Many applications (and companies selling applications) are best-of-breed when purchased, and suddenly the software vendor folds – is acquired, and the software is made legacy – and the software is merged with another product. Or the platform it was developed for goes out of production.

Staying power is one of the subjects of this section. It is critical to make sure today's decisions are valid tomorrow.

IT executives also want successes to demonstrate. A successful project that saves money, or creates opportunity, will help the company as well as improving individual visibility. It creates upward mobility in an organization, as well as adding a potentially important line to a resume.

Speaking of lines on resumes, one of the things that often happen is that pet or pilot projects are defined so the IT executive can add that fascinating new technology onto a line on their resume.

As soon as a new technology gets good press, the savvy CTO/CIO will ask his tech team to check it out. That means an initial trial that is

IT-internal only, followed by identifying a business need that might be met by technology.

At that point, one of two things happen.

Usually, the initial project is moderately successful. However, the consensus is the new technology not only didn't do things much better than the earlier one but now there's an initial project, there are more technologies to maintain, with new applications developed in the more stable, legacy technologies.

The other possibility is the new technology develops roots, is acknowledged to be an improvement over the older technology for overwhelming reasons, and all new development moves in that direction.

Now let's talk about business owners.

Business owners are not just owners of companies. In organizations, business owner refers to the person responsible for a business line, such as budget, profit, and loss.

The business owner doesn't have a preference as to technology, as long as it works.

The business owner wants to maximize revenue and profits.

Business owners will often read technology newsletters, see what the marketing is all about, believe there's an application of the idea, and offer to fund the prototype for the CIO.

Now, we finally turn to technology trends.

For the last 30 years or so, the business technology world has been oriented toward structured data, and more specifically, relational databases. This data architecture has been successful for reasons, not the least of which is a simple language (Structured Query Language – SQL).

So much money has been invested in this technology, chances of it going away anytime soon are negligible. This will continue to be the database technology of choice for the foreseeable future.

That said, there is far more data in the world that is non-structured, and non-structured data is valuable when you can gather, collate, corroborate, analyze and mine data.

What are large quantities of unstructured data?

Let's discuss rush hour traffic through your town. Where are all cars, how fast are they travelling, how crowded are the roads, where are bottlenecks? Which cars are running low on gas, oil and tire tread? Which roads are under construction; what routes are no longer optimal because of any of the above?

This is all unstructured data. In a world where we could process unlimited amounts of unstructured data quickly and efficiently, you could:

- Reroute traffic
- Deploy repair vehicles, tow trucks, emergency vehicles; perhaps even automatically set up road diversion
- Identify which cars are likely to have tire problems and deploy mobile repair vehicles
- Notify vehicle owners they need new tires
- Determine which vehicles need oil changes, or work to optimize performance or mileage.

The problem is the computing power and development time needed to perform these tasks is Herculean. So it's not happening in the near future.

To put a few names and acronyms to unstructured data try Mongo, Hadoop, and NoSQL, the new wave of non-relational databases. Unless your pockets are deep, stick with relational for the time being. A recent successful project I'm aware of took 50 people two years. That's eight figures just in salaries, not counting hardware, software licensing and intangibles.

Hardware technology changes almost continuously. You may have read or heard of "Moore's Law." Postulated about 40 years ago, there are versions which sometimes include computing power and sometimes transistors; it boils down as follows: Computing power doubles every 18 months, and the costs halved.

So, it seems like we'll get there (that is, getting to the big/unstructured data solutions).

Physicists are suggesting rate will decrease, but costs seem to continue to come down.

Storage technology seems to continue to accelerate. Today, the newer flash drives are about 50 times faster than the previous generation of enterprise storage and at a smaller price.

The world is moving to flash storage; it's smaller, faster and much cheaper to run, as it takes less rack space and electricity. In some cases, the savings are enough to pay for storage.

The world also is moving toward the cloud. This is software as a service; this is hosting everything and easy access to fully loaded application development environments. We are going to see more applications for everything and services are going to be improved.

The world is not going to be in the cloud completely. After trials, the business world has ebbed and flowed into and outside the cloud, which will likely continue as companies decide what makes more sense in what circumstances.

Anybody who tells you they know without a doubt where the world is moving is trying to sell you something. These, though, are the trends.

Gartner group predicts these five big data trends.

By 2018 the Gartner group predicts employers will have more smart machines on location than employees. The use of smart machines will be a reduction in overhead while companies with 150 employees or less will be generating $85 to $160 million in revenue. [#15F]

Smart machines help release human controls using algorithmic trading or lights-out operations with factories with no employees. Also, smart machines can augment the knowledge of humans, adding processing power and capabilities.

Voice command, facial and voice recognition in 2018 will help modify and personalize the shopping and maneuvering relationship for customers during interactions with companies. This will enhance and support a more meaningful relationship, increasing potential profitability, and sales for the enterprise.

Internet of things

The Gartner Group said 2016 spending on the Internet will exceed $2.5 million a minute. The GDP will add up to $10 trillion to $15 trillion over the next 20 years. [#15F]

Employment for IT positions including software developers and computer systems engineers has grown between 113 to 215 percent in the past year.

Business content

By 2018, 20 percent of all business content will be authored by machines. The data retrieved for reports, white papers and news releases will be written and presented by computers. The advances in data integration, predictive analytics and empowered computerized writers will allow this to occur.

By 2018, 23 million workers will have Robo-bosses. Evaluations and performance reviews of employees will be happening through automation provided in analytical techniques using computer power.

I am predicting a lot of the data and news sources we will see in the future will come from automated processes. The analysis and predictability used in the corporate structure also will be utilized in social and news media campaigns. Eventually, the data will be self-driven and self-motivated. As people create more queries and add logic to processes, computers will learn what we want and when we want it. They will provide personalized information based on our profile that has been learned as we navigate the Internet, shop, read and learn. Eventually, everything we see will be what we want to know, react to, shop for or learn. The responsibility will be on us to be more open minded, well rounded and to respond to information that is shared with us to ensure we don't become a self-censured society. The dialogue between individuals may be more necessary and more thought-provoking than ever before.

Data warehousing

In the old days, data storage was expensive. We remember a project that was justified based on the cost of storage: a 65-gigabyte "demographics research" database (this would now be called a data warehouse) was built on a middle tier because the cost of storage ($2k/gig) was cheaper than on the mainframe ($40K/gig).

As of this writing, you can get flash storage (fast, persistent, solid state) for $1.25/gig in quantity.

The idea behind data warehousing is to understand the data you have collected so you can access customers more profitably. You also can store human resource data to look at historical records to discern current and past productivity, and evaluate information to increase morale and profitability. A data warehouse can be used to store competitor's information so you can incorporate strategies and go to marketing campaigns to win over more share.

The implementation of a data warehouse gathers information from your transactional database and aggregates it in a manner useful to your business – often on a time axis, and with many characteristics.

You probably use your data for a variety of purposes, such as taking orders, maintaining inventory and invoicing customers.

Have you ever thought about using your client's order data to identify buying patterns to increase revenue? Retailers use the information they collect on purchases to improve revenue based on merchandise people often buy together. For example, if you go to Walmart and buy a DVD, chances are you're going to see microwave popcorn and Snowcaps by the cash register because people often buy candy and popcorn with their movies.

After a company is established, the data warehouse uses Big Data for analysis in the marketplace, and it can make decisions faster. Enterprises that use Big Data analysis can find market trends they can quickly take advantage of.

Business owners and managers should be designers of the data warehouse project. Sharing with IT staff means letting them know what data you want to store and how you want to process it. What reports you want? How long you need to keep data. What should be stored in the data warehouse and what can be archived to get out of the way? When building the data warehouse, you should consider rules determining what is stored and for how long. This data is intended to be kept, and long term and will grow, but you may want to consider creating a rule to clean out data past a specified date. If you need it all, then create the rule, but you may want to re-evaluate as time goes on.

To properly create a data warehouse, you need to use correct tools. Investing in high-quality data replication resources and proper storage is a must. Evaluate storage based on cost and usability of space on devices. Some devices state they have X gigabytes available but once machines are up and running with the software needed to run them, a lot of space is used.

How do I begin?

Business leaders should come together and work on definitions. What data can be cleansed; how do you want data presented? What should be included in the data warehouse? What should not?

What are rules and wishes for the team for reporting and analysis? This is the data gathering phase of a project not unlike any other application processes. But the business team that will be providing input may be larger than any other project you worked on, with overlaying thoughts and ideas.

You need to start at the drawing board. Envision what you wish you can get from reports. How do you want reports and data analysis to be presented? Today's technology means you can present data either in lengthy written reports or in graphic images to excite the user.

The second stage is to work with IT to share the vision of the team. Start a more formalized approach to data gathering, allowing the IT staff to create specs, use cases, and business rules to ensure project success. This phase should not be skipped nor half done; if it is not completed well and thoughtfully you will have changes down the road.

When you deploy a data warehouse, you are usually starting from scratch and purchasing hardware, loading system software, and the databases. Then the data is extracted, cleansed and loaded into each of the databases. After the setup is installed, so the data warehouse is accepting specific data from each of its sources, the application processes are installed and set up.

Chapter 16:

Health Care Data, Who Owns It?

Although you may not be a company that controls, stores or owns medical data you are probably a patient and may be interested in this topic with this viewpoint. [#16F]

Only one state defines legal ownership of medical data, and that is New Hampshire. New Hampshire law indicates the final owner of medical data is the patient.

HIPAA and other laws determine the EHR (Electronic Health Records) companies, physicians' medical caretakers, hospitals and other vendors are more like stewards of patient's data. The HIPAA laws state the patient has rights and expectations of privacy, access, and ability to ask for data to be amended should there be an error in reports. The medical professional has to have the capacity to change data. The medical provider can retain both versions of the information.

The physicians and the EHR firms tend to argue over who owns data. In the end, according to HIPAA laws, the doctor owns the data, and the data must be available to them, so they change EHR providers. Also, the data that resides on EHR environment at the end of the contract must be destroyed.

There is a movement to insist physicians share their treatment information with other authorities to help form a medical repository of data that can create methodologies and treatment plans, and this information should be shared in the global medical market. Research clinicians and others would be able to use data to further research and create safer and more efficient health care treatments. Indeed, there is a movement to centralize medical data, and it is getting positive and negative responses from the medical community. Physicians, although they may see value in the ability to profile their patients and run treatment plans that may accurately pinpoint adverse reactions and increase the probability of successful outcomes, recognize the workload for their IT and admin staff having to report treatment plans of all patients to a central repository.

In the end, owners of data are not legal owners, but they are provided with rights and considerations.

Doctors and medical professionals can change the data; they can store and use data for reporting and payment; they need to supply data to the specific agencies, and they must protect the data and make it available to patients. They cannot delete, lose or allow unknown or uninvited sources to have access to it. The patient has expectations the medical provider will honor their responsibilities and help them manage data by sharing history with other doctors and with the hope the doctor will be able to manage treatment plans effectively.

Patients may or may not want data to go into the central medical repository, but they may not have a say in this process. Just as they relinquish rights to allow insurance company providers to have access to information to process billing, they could eventually have to relinquish records so they can have a treatment plan using their demographics and life situations.

One thing for certain, the data age is upon us and the more we know, the more everyone is going to know about us. Our mirrors may one day not only reflect our images but details of our health, medical and social needs as well.

Critical issues here are; you work out data ownership with customers contractually, and you ensure the contract complies with HIPAA laws. [#17F]

Chapter 17

Cloud vs. On Premise Storage

Major technology vendors have stepped up efforts to emphasize benefits of storing data and running applications, platforms and infrastructure in the cloud, whether public or private. But many IT leaders I speak with as a consultant remain caught in the debate over maintaining on-premises data centers vs. moving to the cloud.

The cynic in us asks why they want to do that. Answers frequently point to money or control …and sometimes control means money. There is a lot of licensing value in storing data, which is hard to relocate once contained/stored, and is excellent collateral. A cloud is usually a physical server that holds multiple virtual servers. You share the resources on these servers with one to many other applications. It is possible that you don't even know where your server is located. You could hold a contract with a local company that is licensing everything from IP addresses to space and software licenses from a third party in another part of the country, or the world. If you store Personal Information (see the Security chapter), you may want to ask your cloud provider where your virtual server will be and the type of data mix you will have. Your data on the hardware is not stored on different disks or separate data sectors. Your data on the equipment could be intermixed. Plus, the performance of the server can be affected by the usage of your fellow tenants. Should they have a transaction that runs out of control, it could cause CPU or i/o issues which slow up your application response for your employees and customers. Your needs will determine whether you should consider a dedicated server just for your company's use, as well as the host's data protection processes. You should also ask if you can be placed on a server with fellow HIPPA compliant organizations, etc. **#10F**)

Here are some reasons to keep your data on the site:

Regulations and specific business requirements

Depending on industry sector, vertical market or geographical location, you may have to abide by government regulations determining how you use and store sensitive data. The healthcare and financial services industries are examples where the government is extraordinarily intrusive in requirements – perhaps rightly so, as some institutions have not protected data well. This may require keeping sensitive data stored in private data centers. However, many organizations are turning to the cloud As mentioned, ask a lot of questions about the type of tenants, action that could be taken that could correct any performance issues and ask them to help you decide whether you should be on a dedicated cloud server. Also, don't forget that some of the regulations require you to use supported software and hardware versions and that updates and patches are applied as required by the vendors. Therefore, make sure you go over all of your requirements with your cloud provider and come up with a plan to stay industry compliant.

Security

While you can make the case that cloud vendors have better security measures than most private companies, individual companies are dealing with data that requires more advanced security than what cloud providers can offer. Executives also may feel comfortable shouldering risk themselves. (Other officials use that reason for the opposite reason – pushing the blame to someone else in case of a breach.) In both instances, security can be a determining factor in choosing to store data and apps on premises. The specific questions to ask are: what is the profile of the other tenants on the server, do you have servers dedicated to protecting PI information, who is responsible for backing up my data? Where are the backups located? Hopefully not on the same server. What if this server goes down, do you have replication or always on (mirroring) set up, so our application will be up and running in x minutes, hours or days?

If I want to backup to hardware outside of your cloud? What costs would I incur, for instance, if my back up is x size and takes y hours what would the throughput costs? You want to have a backup of your data, vital code, databases, etc. on premise in a locked box. The cost of getting those backups pushed to your hardware can affect your budget and be a pain if the throughput is slow.

Once sensitive data is moved or generated on a public cloud, it becomes difficult to see where the data resides. Meaning that as mentioned before your data is not stored in its only little sector on a disk. It is stored on the disk with other organizations data unless you ask for your dedicated cloud server. (Which is the same as having your hardware dedicated to your use only)

Accessibility

Is not much different than how would set up in an on-premise device. If you have direct connections between specific clients, then you may be able to set up a WAN (Wide Area Network), but if you are using the internet, then accessibility is determined between the i/o you request from the cloud provider and then the end client who is running the application. Some days the internet inherently runs slow because there is a lot of traffic. Or if you are in an office where there are a lot of reports being downloaded from the cloud server you may see slower application and data response times. You can control this problem by adding more throughput on both ends from the cloud to your home office. The costs can be significant so watch your budget and make sure you know how much this will cost before you ask for it.

Vendor relationship

Remember this is a vendor/client relationship. Your connection with your cloud provider is as close to the life blood of your company as the surgeon is to your body. You should check the provider out closely. Ask questions about their longevity, financial stability, and their experience with working with the regulations in your industry. Discuss and make sure that they can meet the requirements of your industry. In the end, the data controls are your responsibility. If the cloud provider contractually can protect your data as you need, then you can pass the buck a bit, but you still must plan for all forms of disasters. Working closely with your provider can help you create a full blanket of protection for your data. However, you can't be lazy; you must work on that relationship, reconnect once a year. Review your full data protection plans with them and work together to fill in the holes.

Now let's flip it around: Why go cloud?

Flexibility and fast start up

Cloud based services can allow you to quickly add space and bandwidth. The only thing you need to bring is your check book. They can usually make the adjustments in hours or days depending on your needs. A cloud server can be available to you in hours if you are a small company with small data space requirements. This fast entry to the technology can save you a lot in start-up costs and accelerate the time when you first open your doors. Many large companies are moving to the cloud for the same reasons. As they grow they need to be very pliable, and they are considering the costs of building their own on-premise data center and deciding "sharing the rent," and being able to get started on new projects or adding bandwidth is a lot faster and less expensive when going to the cloud.

Disaster recovery

You should ask what they have available, use it, test it. No one can protect you 100% from hackers, hardware failures or acts of god and weather. Most data centers take advantage of high-availability, mirroring or replication. One of the most important factors is to make sure that you can back up your application code, data and databases to a site your team can access should the worst happen to the cloud service provider.

Don't forget to verify that you can restore not only your data but your application code. Also, verify and don't assume that all of the required hardware and software patches are being applied to your cloud server. Part of disaster recovery is planning and prevention. Force yourself to undergo a security audit even if your industry doesn't require it and include your cloud provider in that process.

Losses incurred from having your systems and applications inaccessible by your clients can revert to millions per minute. Plus, if you do have HIPPA data then you could incur fines if the information is not readily available. Lastly, losing your own proprietary code will bring tears to the eyes of many of your team members.

Cost of entry

The costs to original entry can save you a lot of money. You will be sharing hardware costs with other organizations; you avoid costly licensing fees of a lot of software from the firewall to server to some application software. You save money on the data access through the shared pipe. The largest savings may be in personnel and floor space. You don't have to find a locked climate controlled room with personnel with different technical abilities to keep your systems up and running. Plus, that headache is someone else's so you can blame them for your issues and not carry the stress on your shoulders.

Physical security

There is a lot of potential savings for you here. You do not need a specialized climate controlled locked room with high-level security measures and employee access protocols to worry about. You won't need to add to a person's job description to collect the key or change the passwords anytime the need arises. One less thing for you to worry about during security audits or day to day activities. Secondly purchasing all the software and setting up the hardware properly to protect your data, has a lot of costs associated. Third, you are saving on a lot of technical human power. Lastly, the cloud provider daily reviews information regarding any intrusions that may happen and will patch your hardware and software to keep the bad guys out. This means they test the patches first on different environments and then post them to production. This process alone can save you time and heartache.

Chapter 18

Database Performance for Executives

We received a call recently from a business partner who told us, "We have a customer, a large hospital, who complained of database performance issues. We spent $3 million of their money upgrading systems and performance remains the same. The CIO is worried about his job, and we are worried we are going to be sued for the $3 million. Can you help us?"

This one incident indicates a host of problems. First and foremost, to solve a problem, you have to identify it. This premise sounds simple, but I assure you it is common to throw hardware at a problem. The problem is if the hardware was not your problem, hardware wouldn't solve it. This is intuitive after the fact, but you also must understand the issue of making changes in database production environments.

While onsite at a large health insurance company a few years ago, the firm had a relatively small window, six weeks, to attempt a database upgrade. At any organization of any size, a database upgrade is something you test before putting it into production. At this customer site, there was a performance issue in the new software they'd uncovered. A process taking about two minutes, which was barely acceptable, was suddenly taking 23 minutes, which was unacceptable. If they could solve it, they could roll out (internally certify and upgrade the software.). If not, they'd have to wait almost a year for the next window.

In comes the expert, us. We found while they identified a particular software bug, there was another option. The code was miswritten (in fact, it was one reason the bug was uncovered). A small change in code and the two-minute job could run in 2 microseconds. Pleased with the finding, we brought it to the customer expecting a pat on the head, only to have the client tell me the solution was unacceptable. With a six-week window, I had expected this would be an easy code change to fix and roll in and was surprised my solution was rejected. After all, this was about 60,000 times faster than the prior approach, and 600,000 times faster than their existing dilemma. The customer said, "It takes us eight weeks to review and roll out any changes. Try again."

The message here is for IT executives; it is easier – politically and technologically – to make a hardware change than a software change. CIOs often throw money at a problem to make it go away because it is more cost effective to guarantee an immediate resolution to a problem than to identify root cause and fix it.

The catch is, if the problem wasn't hardware, it might be that faster CPUs, more memory, or faster storage access times are not what was needed. That health insurance company found out the hard way. Sometimes you have no alternative to fixing code or tuning the database.

This is one place where there is no substitution for experience and expertise – note those are two separate, mandatory requirements.

Root cause analysis

To solve a problem, you first need to identify the problem. Buying faster hardware may address the problem if in fact there is one. But this approach simply masks the problem for a while; the problem continues to snowball, then the snowball freezes and hits you with an ice ball instead of a fluffy one.

So, how do we get there from here?

Tools

First, you need tools that enable you to measure what's happening on your system. There are dozens of tools, and most of them are junk. I've lost count of the number of times I've been brought in to solve a performance problem, proudly shown tools the shop has purchased but which are useless and the reason they couldn't figure out the problem without us.

We will not be listing tools here. We don't want to catch flak from vendors, and while we are reselling the few tools we believe are good, meaning make us successful, we change those over time, and would much rather ask for a recommendation.

That said, your tool needs to do many things:

1.) Measure utilization of resources over time. CPU, memory (different from CPU), storage bandwidth, network bandwidth. That list of four is a simplification, as there are multiple metrics that are tracked for each, but it's the starting list.
2.) Measure impact of database activity. This includes ability to identify which queries are running, and what they are doing. "What they are doing" in this context does not mean what report they are running, but what resources they are using and how they are using them. For example, it's important to know if a query is CPU-bound (limited by CPU), memory-bound or blocked by another process with locks on it.
3.) Measure impact of other activities as they interact. "Is my report slow because lots of folks are running it because it's being blocked, or because I simply can't push that much data over the Internet?"
4.) Graphically and quickly identify which queries are taking up most resources.
5.) Graphically and easily identify which queries are taking up most elapsed time.
6.) Graphically and easily identify which queries are running most frequently.

      a.   There's a difference between one query running for an hour and one query running once per second for an hour and one query running 1,000 times/second for an hour

7.) Graphically and easily identify which logins are involved in the above, critical in tracking down who did what and when.

There's more, but this is a start. If your tool can't do these things, and it's simply enough a production support manager (manager and not data expert) can look, identify a problem, and ask for resolution, your tool likely lives on a shelf and doesn't get used.

Fixing the underlying problems

So once you've identified the underlying problem, that's where you target resources, whether it be buying hardware or something else. As of now, the most frequent hardware purchases we recommend are faster disk – for when we have positively quantified an IO bandwidth issue – and memory, also when we've quantified an issue. Most folks overbuy CPU as it's a commodity today, even with DBMS vendors pricing their wares by CPU.

Before we do either of those, though, we look to tune the application. It's not unusual, with a few relatively minor and straightforward changes, to reduce CPU from 95 percent to 16 percent (a recent success), or memory requirements to a tiny percentage of what they were, or disk requests from 100 trillion/hour to 3,000/hour. We are not making that one up either.

Note, research organizations have quantified mean time to resolution, or MTTR, for performance issues at 80 percent identification of problem, 20 percent resolution. It's another reason to invest in a tool to track down issues.

How do we do this? There are three primary tasks: query tuning, architecture and index selection.

Query tuning

What happens in real life (that is, outside the classroom) is the fact software developers are good at creating logical, sensible, procedural code relatively easy to maintain. This last part is important. CIOs/ CTOs will tell you average cost of maintenance of an application is seven times cost of developing it. Restated, if you spend $1 million building a software application, you'll spend $7 million maintaining it before the application gets replaced. The easier the code is to maintain, the lower you can keep that number because business rules and needs always change.

Here's your problem: The people who write your applications do not understand database performance, and as a result often create artistic examples of sophistry. They are creations which are logical but flawed because they don't understand how the underlying technology works.

Solution: have your DBAs code review before any data manipulation language, or DML, accesses anything on your production database applications.

Architecture

The architecture of your DBMS is hardware and application dependent, but there are issues that can negatively drive performance. Here's a short list.

High availability is a buzz phrase that has made the circuit and means if your primary DBMS fails, you have another one to back it up, often automatically. For example, if primary server is in Miami, and Miami gets hit by a hurricane, are your users in Chicago going to be happy the hurricane, which perhaps cut off power or an Internet line, means they are unable to do their jobs?

There are ways you can make this happen, many of them popular and fruitful today. Some of them are being done, though, with eye toward perfection rather than performance.

For example, let's say you have a primary data center in Miami, with a failover in Chicago. It's reasonable to assume a hurricane hitting Miami won't take out the Chicago data center and an ice storm taking out the Chicago data center is going to have no effect on Miami. The good decision so far.

Have you considered, though, the speed of light? How is that relevant?

Well, pushing information across a fast line to Chicago from Miami might take 30ms. The signal coming back that says "Got it!" would take the same 30ms; 60ms round trip time doesn't seem like a lot. In fact, as an exercise for the reader, wait 60ms before you read this next sentence. Wait, 60ms is a bit below our threshold of awareness but multiply that by thousands of processes per second. This might end up creating a backlog which affects performance on primary server.

That example assumed "synchronous" data commitment – in other words, making a change at the one site could not complete before the change was made permanent at the remote site. What, though, if we chose "asynchronous" data commitment? For asynchronous commitment, we commit or make permanent, changes on the primary, without regard to whether the secondary is up, and trust changes to make it to the secondary. It becomes possible there's a lag between data on the primary moving to the secondary, in case of a sudden unavailability of the primary and failover to the secondary, of about 30 ms of data.

Some places and times, this is no matter. Users will know there was a failover, and make sure whatever they were working on made it. Others, that loss is unacceptable. For example, you are transferring money from checking to savings account, and an automatic withdrawal fails because of that, your payments are late and don't make it. There will be lots of unhappy campers.

Indexing

Indexing is lifeblood of the database performance expert.

We hope you're old enough to remember phone books, as we haven't come up with a better metaphor for database b-tree indexes. (Binary Tree indexes are an old term no longer used because the indexes are no longer binary.)

Consider the phone book. It is an index organized by last name, first name, middle name, which allows you to look up an address and telephone number.

This phone book structure is key to getting information quickly from large databases.

Consider a table with 100 million rows of data in it. This is not the least bit unusual anymore. A 100 million used to be a large table, but we have customers with 20 employees with much larger tables, on the order of 10 to 100 times bigger. So, how do you want to find your address and phone number? By checking every row? Or by using the phone book? We will pick the phone book most of the time (not all the time; this is where database performance experts earn their money) as we can get to the information we want with just a few (8-10) page requests (a page is the basic unit of io, or input/output), rather than millions.

That telephone book (or the indexes) are going to need to be constructed to meet needs of each query that runs against the database. Stated technically, any query the DBMS needs to optimize, and process will need a matching index to avoid table scan – the systematic scanning of the entire table.

Matching the indexes to queries is a science and art, and can affect query performance. An example is reducing a 48-hour query to 23 seconds by modifying an index.

Case Summary

A partner referred a hosting company (for physician billing and records data) to us. Upon analysis, we were able to add many indexes and reduce workload on the server to approximately 30% of the prior server load.

The operational people were happy, but the physicians still were not, because the queries that were bringing up patient records were still taking about 11 seconds. Doctors are known for their patients, not their patience, and our new client was facing the potential loss of several of their customers, so they asked us back in to look at the specific query.

We pointed a database performance tool at the server and ran the query. We found that about a third of the query was spent in an "io wait" state – that is, waiting for io to be performed. As the queries were already tuned, the only way to make that faster (it was a 3rd-party application, re-architecture wasn't an option) would be faster storage.

An AFA (all flash array) took io wait out of the issue, but buffer wait accounted for another third of the elapsed time. In other words, bringing the pages into cache from the disk was also excessive. This required more memory. Once both hardware issues were resolved, performance was about 2.5 seconds, making everybody very happy.

Note that calls to the vendor gleaned the information that 11 seconds was about the best they've seen… leading us to believe the vendor didn't understand database performance, identification and elimination of bottlenecks, or general customer service.

Summary

There are a lot of factors in database performance, some of which we've discussed here. Physical resources are a component, but we've seen over the years hundreds of situations where throwing hardware at a problem not only didn't solve it but sometimes temporarily masked it and created other problems, often more urgent.

Get expertise early, when you expect your business to be growing, or your data volumes to be dramatically changing.

Chapter 19

How do we Protect our Data Warehouse

If at all possible the data warehouse should be set up in its environment, where you have controlled access for data insertions, as well as separate and distinct hardware for loads and queries. Data should only come from specific devices/IP addresses.

It also is common to encrypt your data. That way if your storage device is stolen, data is likely protected.

Data warehouses also must be maintained; the software will need bug fixes and possible upgrades. The hardware must be maintained and protected as well. Performance and capacity analysis must be performed routinely. The entire data warehouse system should be backed up and replicated in case of a disaster caused by hardware or software corruption, or flood or fire. Proper firewalls and other strategies need to be set up to keep out unwanted access, to stop worms, SQL injections or ransomware attacks.

As you set forth on your data warehouse project make sure you have planned and budgeted to protect the asset.

Chapter 20

Getting the Right Data?

When gathering data, one of the first things you want to decide is how information will be collected. If the approach is skewed or problematic in nature, the data will be of no use at best. At worst, the approach can lead you astray, costing your company valuable capital. Any form of collecting data can be compared to a survey, whether it's from an insurance employee filling out a claim form, or a customer ordering a product online. In this section, I will be approaching the subject from perspective of surveying, for the purpose of being able to provide examples. The two questions to ask yourself when deciding how to aggregate the information are: "What should be asked?" and "What medium should I use?" This chapter will go over points where many people would typically falter.

What is a wrong question/ Avoid skewing data by asking the wrong question

There are two ways a question can be wrong. The first is asking the question in a way that you cannot use the information the question would lead to; the second is if information is skewed.

In the U.S. General Social Survey, individuals were asked: "Do you think the law should forbid marriages between blacks and whites?" or "Do you think the law should allow marriages between blacks and whites?" When asked the former, 19 percent of respondents said yes. However, when asked the latter, 31 percent of respondents said no. Concisely speaking, 19 percent of people surveyed wished to forbid interracial marriage, but 31 percent wish to disallow it.

Logically speaking, since forbid and allow are antonyms, you would think the two numbers would be similar, if not equal, since they mean the same thing – both would render interracial marriage illegal. This is an example of the effect wording of a question has on the answer. Because forbid has such a harsh connotation, people would have stronger convictions to say yes than they would disagree with "allowing" it. In other words, people on the fence about this issue did not approve of interracial marriage but forbid sounded too drastic.

Let's look at an example of this principle that may apply to a small business. Say you were looking to open a family-owned pharmacy in a moderate-sized town, Peopleton. Your town has the pharmacy chains C-greens and WVS, but you'd like to see if residents of Peopleton would be open to patronizing a pharmacy with fewer hours and slightly higher prices. In exchange, residents would get more personal service and knowledge their money would go back into the community, instead of going to a corporation.

You've decided to survey to gauge interest. Your first instinct may be to word the question like this: "Would you rather support a large corporate chain than a local family-run business?" However, you'd be hard pressed to find someone who would answer yes to that question without at least some hesitation. The skew in that question is two-fold; first of all, since one option is "family-run" the average person would look at the other option as "not family" or "anti-family" and therefore less wholesome Secondly, by describing the chain as large, you've painted the local business as the underdog.

A better question may be: "Are you open to switching pharmacies?" Although the question may seem less specific, it is more so, since now you are asking about the proper industry and will likely provide accurate results with same meaning.

The next kind of bad question is one you cannot use the answer for, either because it is too open-ended, too off-topic or both. To stick with the pharmacy example, at first, it may seem like a good idea to ask a question such as, "Describe the best experience you've ever had at a pharmacy," while hoping you could use answers to make those experiences shared in your establishment. Unfortunately, while analyzing results of a survey, you will have dozens of results to skim through. Variation of answers will likely be huge since no two can be the same. In short, the data from that question would be impossible to compile, and likely useless.

A better alternative would be "describe the most important feature of a pharmacy in one word." However the variation would be quite significant, and data may be difficult to analyze without a huge population.

An ideal question would be: "Which of the following qualities is the most important to you in a pharmacy: price, timeliness, cleanliness, friendliness, professionalism." Those answers would be direct, easily quantified, and most importantly it'll tell you what potential customers want you to prioritize in your business.

Getting the data

The biggest, most expensive survey system in the world will not help if you aren't using the right method for your target demographic. This exact point was demonstrated best by Literary Digest in 1936. In one of the most famous publishing blunders of the 20th century, the well-respected magazine printed the most inaccurate prediction of a major public opinion poll recorded. It was an election year, and the race was between Democratic incumbent Franklin D. Roosevelt and Republican Alfred Landon. Using for the first time telephones to poll Americans, the Literary Digest predicted Landon would win the election, taking 370 electoral votes and about 57 percent of the popular vote. Nearly 2.4 million people responded to their survey, giving them an enormous sample size and implying the data should be relatively accurate. To their disbelief, when results came to pass, it was Roosevelt who won, with 61 percent of the vote, and all but eight electoral votes. It is commonly accepted the cause of this was their use of telephone polling before telephones were in most American households. [#19F]

Using the latest and greatest technology ensured people answering those phones would be those who could afford such commodities during the Great Depression. Roosevelt at the time was pushing his New Deal which was aimed at helping those in the lower class. Naturally, people who are less affected by the policy would be less impressed, and therefore less likely to vote for him.

The lesson of this story is your method of gathering information has to reflect the information you need.

What is an outlier?

An important thing to be able to determine when collecting data is which pieces do not fit together, and more importantly how to tell the difference between data that is probably wrong or tainted vs. data that's unusually high. Determining whether a piece of data is an outlier is an effective method. An outlier is mathematically defined as a number more than 1.5 times the interquartile range from the appropriate quartile. To explain this concept, let's look at an example. You are trying to determine how long it takes for a customer to purchase an item from your company's website so that abnormal purchases can be marked in the database for review. So far, there have been 11 purchases with times in seconds of:

245, 382, 58, 264, 312, 627, 341, 278, 515, 176, 262

The first thing you want to do may be to determine what outliers are to see what went wrong and to do that you will want to determine which numbers are outliers. To begin with, the numbers must be put in order.

58, 176, 245, 262, 264, 278, 312, 341, 382, 515, 627

Then you must determine the median. The median, once the data is sorted, is the number in the exact middle; in this case, it's 278. With this, you can split the data into two halves.

58, 176, 245, 262, 264 and 312, 341, 382, 515, 627

Next, find the quartiles. To do that, you find the median of each half of the data; in this case, 245 and 382. The median of the lower half of the data, 245, is called the first quartile and the median of the higher set is called the third quartile. (The second quartile is the real median.)

Next, you want to find the interquartile range, which is third quartile minus the first, and then multiply it by 1.5.

382-245 = 137

137x1.5 = 205.5

Then you must find the range that determines an outlier by subtracting the 205.5 from the first quartile and adding it to the third.

245-205.5 = 39.5

382+205.5 – 587.5

This means outliers are numbers below 39.5 and above 587.5, meaning the only outlier in this dataset is 627.

At first, glance, when looking at the data, one may assume 58 and 515 also are outliers, which is why finding the actual numbers is necessary. Although there may have been something that went wrong with those two purchases, it is far more likely the order with a time of 627 had an issue. At this point you are probably asking whether or not you have to do this by hand; the answer is no. There are programs on the Internet which will allow you to input data manually, and if you have a large system, it should be simple to create a program to alert you when outliers are recorded.

Who not to ask/what's a target demographic; How people's demographic affects the answer

Before going through steps of creating a business, most people pitch the idea to friends, family, and neighbors hoping to get input on the new project. Since all information is coming from biased sources, none of it can be trusted. What you need is to find opinions of people you plan to sell your idea to; these people are your target demographic.

An anecdote; Also, who to ask and how to ask the right question

If you are having difficulty figuring out who is your target demographic, think about the use of your product specifically. Then think about who would have that need and the income, and then figure out how to describe them as a group. Sometimes that may require research.

As an example, let's say you have just invented the dishwasher. Naturally, it washes a large number of dishes at a time. A bachelor living alone probably doesn't own enough dishes to fill it, and may not be bothered by washing a single plate and cup each night to spend hundreds on a washing machine. Your target demographic would describe a person who often washes dishes for several people, and has funds for your new contraption. In most cases, that would be a married woman with children old enough whose husband has stable disposable income.

That is not to say some single women won't buy it, or no married men do dishes, but the idea of finding your demographic is describing most of the people you are selling to as accurately and specifically as possible. If you look at advertisements for dishwashers, you will see major companies agree; they almost exclusively feature women who either have children in the advertisement or appear to be in their mid-20s.

Using another example, if you wish to sell customized golf clubs, so the customer will have a unique club. People with a need for an exclusive club would be golfers who play a significant amount and have plenty of disposable income. It may be useful to figure out, at this point, the demographic of people who play golf. If you were to use a simple search engine you'd find statisticbrain.com has done all the work. A mere 17 percent of golfers are below 40. About 77.5 percent are men; they have an average income of $95,000 per year, and nearly 70 percent are married. Accounting for all those facts, your demographic is married men over 40. **xx**

Summary

Putting knowledge into action:

This is all useful for marketing. For example, let's say you are trying to open a new luxury car rental business. First, you would establish a target demographic, people who have licenses, older than 25 (the age people can rent cars in most states), with income high enough to afford your cars. Then you'll want to figure out where to put the business, based on location demographics.

1   After you've narrowed down location ideas, you will want to survey potential renters. You will need to find out what kind of cars to buy, so you will ask questions such as: "Which of the following qualities are most important to you in a rented vehicle: speed, comfort, safety or appearance?" You may be tempted, but don't ask a question such as: "Would you rather drive an amazingly fast and cool car or a safe one?" You also can ask a question such as: "About how much per week would you be willing to spend on a rental car?" You will need to determine the most efficient way to get the survey to your target market to collect opinions. Then you will need to look at price points the potential buyers have written down. You will want to determine the outliers, and remove them from the data, and use the information you have gathered to choose which cars will have space on your lot, and which would have inadequate demand. If you follow these steps, you'll be well on your way to having a reliable clientele.

Afterward

We hope this book helped you gain a new perspective about how important data is to your company concerning your role as a business manager.

The themes in this book should help you evaluate the intrinsic and also the actual real monetary value of data. We also hope we have presented different issues to consider and given you the ability to analyze data and develop plans to protect it.

We hope first you ask, then answer, these questions: How much data can you afford to lose? What data can be reconstructed if it is lost? What data is necessary to keep your company running? Who owns the data? How much of the data belongs to an individual? Are we following laws in all our global regions? Can we report we are following proper procedures to protect the data?

Then ask yourself, do I have sufficient maintenance, security and backup plans that will protect data through storms?

If the answer is "I cannot afford to lose even an hour's worth of data" then you have to ask yourself are backups occurring every 15 minutes and are we logging transactions to cover the 14 minutes between full backups?

If my systems cannot be down for minutes or hours, do I have High Availability or other processes in place, so if this environment goes down for hardware, software or data corruption failure we can go over to another environment quickly to keep the company up and running.

Are my systems healthy? Is the environment healthy? Are my fail-over processes up and ready to work? You answer these questions by making sure maintenance and alerting jobs are running.

If you need to protect an individual's data, then you will need to look at rules and regulations and review your security processes. Do you review accessibility for employees or other users who should have been closed out of the environment? Do you have encryption used for data passing from database to the user web interface? Do databases need to be encrypted? Who makes sure your code for interface, database, security and web hosting is stored safely and backed up in case you have an internal corrupter or an outside hacker infecting your systems? Or make sure your code is in-house and not all on the developer in either Wisconsin or India's desk laptop?

Would you have ever believed your internal data could be a source of revenue? That is done by looking at details in the data, finding ways to take the data and make it marketable. Actually, is it like bringing gold bullion-like value to the millions of lines of data in all your databases? Is your data accurate? Can you verify the accuracy and while you are reviewing your reports are you asking the right questions? Can you create Use Cases with a clear understanding to make sure you are asking the question to get the correct answer in return?

Can you imagine the day when regulations may eat up more of your IT costs than expected? When that day comes, you will need to create an annual review to see what is coming through legislation and how those requirements will affect the bottom line.

Lastly, don't let the data waste time, energy, human resources, and storage; clean house once in a while and make room for more by purging the old stuff stored in the back hollows of the database server environment.

Bibliography

1F: The value of data and gold, Statistics Canada Website, ©1998 last updated 2013

http://www.statcan.gc.ca/cdu/power-pouvoir/ch1/definitions/5214853-eng.htm

2F: Gantz L, David, USA GOLD, "Gold Seizure USA, ©1997

http://www.usagold.com/gildcdopinion/gold-confiscation-ganz.html

3F: Export.GOV:, © last updated 2017

"Safe Harbor" http://2016.export.gov/SAFEHARBOR/

A: Gov.U.K. "UK. Data Protection"

https://www.gov.uk/data-protection/the-data-protection-act

4F: Mcdonald, Lynn; http://www.chron.com,

http://smallbusiness.chron.com/role-data-business-20405.htmlMany articles here on data management, data and business growth

5F: Marr, Bernard; Forbes, "How Big Data Is Changing Healthcare, "April 21, 2015

http://www.forbes.com/sites/bernardmarr/2015/04/21/how-big-data-is-changing-healthcare/#7e4273c532d9

6F: Rosenbush, Stephen; and Totty, Michael; "How Big Data is changing the World," Wall Street Journal, March 10, 2013

http://www.wsj.com/articles/SB1000142412788732417890457834 0071261396666

7F: Cell Phones In Africa: Communication Lifeline

   http://www.pewglobal.org/2015/04/15/ cell-phones-in-africa-communication-lifeline/

8F: Turkel, Dan; Protect Data Against Ransomware

   A. "Victims Paid Over 24 Million in Ransom in 2016 And That IS Just The Beginning", Business Insider, April 7, 2016

   http://www.businessinsider.com/ doj-and-dhs-ransomware-attacks-government-2016-4

   B. **Ozment, Andy,** "Protect Your Data Against Ransomware," Cybersecurity and Communication Secretary, Assistant. April 6 2016

   https://www.dhs.gov/blog/2016/04/06/ protect-your-data-against-ransomware

   C. FBI NEWS, April 29, 2016

   https://www.fbi.gov/news/stories/ incidents-of-ransomware-on-the-rise

   D. US CERT: United States Computer Readiness Team 2016
   https://www.us-cert.gov/ncas/tips/ST06-008

   E: Protecting Your Networks from Ransomware, DOWNLOAD FROM JUSTICE.GOV

   https://www.justice.gov/criminal-ccips/file/872771/download

9F: Encryption Key Size

https://en.wikipedia.org/wiki/Key_size

10F: Rashid, Fahmida Y, "Cloud Computing"

A. "Dirty Dozen Cloud Security Threats," Info World, March 11, 2016

http://www.infoworld.com/article/3041078/security/the-dirty-dozen-12-cloud-security-threats.html

B. **Luke, Dejun,** "Top Cloud Computing Threats and Vulnerabilities-enterprise environments," Cloud Tech, November 21, 2014

C. http://www.cloudcomputing-news.net/news/2014/nov/21/top-cloud-computing-threats-and-vulnerabilities-enterprise-environment/

11F: Mar, Bernard HIPAA Compliance Checklist

http://www.hipaajournal.com/hipaa-compliance-checklist/

A: Mar, Bernard, Forbes, "How Big Data Is Changing Healthcare" Forbes, April 21, 2015

http://www.forbes.com/sites/bernardmarr/2015/04/21/how-big-data-is-changing-healthcare/#7e4273c532d9

12F: TV Tropes: "9 out of 10 Doctors Agree."

http://tvtropes.org/pmwiki/pmwiki.php/Main/NineOutOfTenDoctorsAgree

13F: Brown, Meta; Forbes "Want to Make Money with Your Data?"

"Want to Make Money with Your Data, FORBES. COM" February 12 20`6 http://www.forbes.com/sites/metabrown/2016/02/26/want-to-make-money-with-your-data-do-this-first/2/#5386d5235038

A: **Booth, David,** "Turning Data into Dollars 3 Stages to Activate Your Data," Marketingland.com, April 27th 2015

http://marketingland.com/turning-data-dollars-3-stages-activate-uour-data-125770

B: "How to Turn Data Into Cash," May 5 2105

https://www.codefuel.com/blog/how-to-turn-data-into-cash/

C: **Ross, Duncan**, From Big Data Big Money, "How to convert Information into Revenue," Computer World UK, March 13 2015

http://www.computerworlduk.com/it-vendors/from-big-data-big-money-how-convert-information-into-revenue-3601651/.

D: "How Big Data Changes the World. World Economic Forum," no author cited December 1, 2015

https://www.weforum.org/agenda/2015/12/how-is-big-data-going-to-change-the-world/

E: **Rosenbush, Stephen, and Totty, Michael** "How Big Data is Changing the Whole Equation for Business, "The Wall Street Journal, March 10 2013

http://www.wsj.com/articles/SB10001424127887324178904578340071261396666

14F: Enforcement and Data

Technology and Security

A: "AT&T is Making Millions Selling Your Phone Records To The Police," Popular Mechanics.com Avery Thompson, Oct 26, 2016 http://www.popularmechanics.com/technology/security/a23567/att-phone-records-police/

B: "Police Used Facebook and Twitter to Track Down Protestors," Fortune.com, author not sighted, October 11, 2016

http://fortune.com/2016/10/11/police-facebook-twitter-data-protesters/

C: **Wyllie, Doug,** "How is Big Data Helping Law Enforcement," Police One.Com, August 20, 2013

https://www.policeone.com/police-products/software/Data-Information-Sharing-Software/articles/6396543-How-Big-Data-is-helping-law-enforcement/

D: **Mor, Yaniv,** "Big Data and Law Enforcement: "Was Minority Report Right?"

https://www.wired.com/insights/2014/03/big-data-law-enforcement-minority-report-right/

14F: **Khan, Michael,** "NSA ends surveillance tactic that pulled in citizen's emails, texts," IT World, April 28, 2017

http://www.itworld.com/article/3193406/security/nsa-ends-surveillance-tactic-that-pulled-in-citizens-emails-texts.html

Foreign Intelligence Surveillance Act 702; FISA 702 (PDF TO DOWNLOAD)

http://intelligence.house.gov/fisa-702/

15F: Jeevan, Manu; "Gartner Group Predicts Five Data Trends," Big Data Made Simple, January 20 2016, bigdata-madesimple.com/gartner-predicts-five-big-data-trends-that-will-dominate-2016/

16F: "Who owns health care data?" Wireless Life Sciences Alliance, September 15 2015

wirelesslifesciences.org/2015/09/who-owns-your-health-care-ehr-data/

A; Who Owns Your Medical Records; 50-State Comparison (REFERENCE INFORMATION)

www.healthinfolaw.org/comparative-analysis/who-owns-medical-records-50-state-comparison

17 F: HIPAA Reference information

https://www.hhs.gov/sites/default/fi1les/privacysummary.pdf

18F: Schwaber, Ken and Sutherland, Jeff, Reference material for scrum" July 2013

http://www.scrumguides.org/docs/scrumguide/v1/scrum-guide-us.pdf

19F: U.S. History on the Web:

"The Poll That Changed Polling," History Matters, Literary Digest, October 31 1936

http://historymatters.gmu.edu/d/5168/

Some research links you might like to read:

- **Statistics CANADA, Power from Data**
  http://www.statcan.gc.ca/edu/power-pouvoir/ch1/
  definitions/5214853-eng.htm
- **How Big Data is Changing Healthcare**
  https://www.forbes.com/sites/bernardmarr/2015/04/21/
  how-big-data-is-changing-healthcare/#11501ab82873
- **Introduction to Data Driven Decisions for Managers Who Don't Like Math**
  https://hbr.org/2014/05/an-introduction-to-data-driven-decisions-
  for-managers-who-dont-like-math
- **Cell Phones In Africa: Communication Lifeline**
  http://www.pewglobal.org/2015/04/15/
  cell-phones-in-africa-communication-lifeline/

Learning about statistics online

- http://stattrek.com/

Battle over her Data

http://www.forbes.com/sites/medidata/2016/03/01/
who-owns-patient-data/#3c24f89c46d6

http://medicaleconomics.modernmedicine.com/
medical-economics/news/battle-over-ehr-patient-data?page=full

EXTRA REFERENCE MATERIALS

Database Management Checklist: Go to www.soaringeagle.biz

Data collection Reference Material: https://drive.google.com/file/d/0B-DHaDEbiOGkc1RycUtIcUtIelE/view

Pdf from Symantec about Ransomware

http://www.symantec.com/content/en/us/enterprise/media/security_response/whitepapers/the-evolution-of-ransomware.pdf

HIPAA Compliance Checklist

http://www.hipaajournal.com/hipaa-compliance-checklist/

About the authors

They are Penny Garbus, Jeff Garbus, and Gillian Garbus. Jeff Garbus has written 20 books; Penny Garbus co-authored with Jeff about four of the books. This is Gillian Garbus' first entry into publishing.

Jeff and Penny Garbus have been running database consulting companies for more than 23 years. They have had the privilege of working with IT teams all over the world.

Jeff Garbus

Jeff's background includes a Bachelor of Science from Rensselaer Polytechnic Institute and work experience from personal computers to mainframes. He has decades of client/server, Sybase, and Microsoft SQL Server experience, with emphasis on assisting customers in migrating from existing systems to large-scale projects with large databases. He is known in the industry, having spoken at user conferences and user groups since the early 1990s, written articles and columns for magazines, and published 20 books on database management systems. Recently his focus has been on database performance, tuning, monitoring, and reengineering. Jeff has stayed at leading edge of technology and excelled at transferring his knowledge to others. Jeff@soaringeagle.guru

Gillian Garbus

Gillian is attending Florida Polytechnic University studying the technology industry. She brings a fascinating couple of chapters to share her knowledge verifying the quality of the data. She is now an entrepreneur herself starting her first business while in college and writing her book "The Dark Side of Data." gillian@soaringeagle.guru

Penny Garbus

Penny Garbus has been working for in the data management field since leaving college when she worked as a data entry clerk for Pitney Bowes Credit. When she was young, she helped her father by answering the phone and learned from him as his computer consulting company grew. She later ran the training and marketing departments of Northern Lights Software and is the co-founder of Soaring Eagle Consulting, Inc. where she is projects lead for software development for their soon-to-be-released database management software. She also is proud mom of four children. One is with a master's degree in electrical engineering, and three are entrepreneurs growing their organizations. Penny@soaringeagle.guru

Printed in the United States
By Bookmasters